COMPUTERGRAPHIA

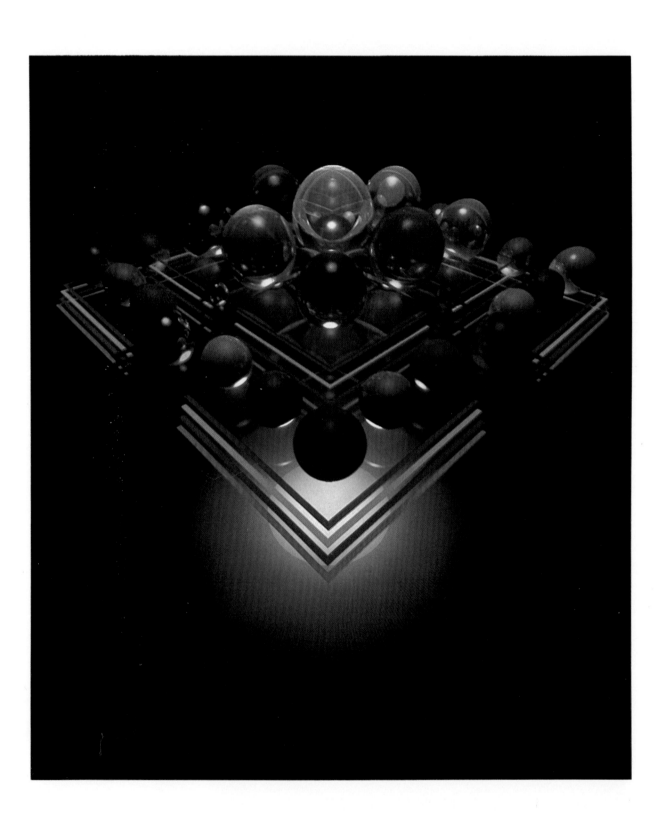

COMPUTERGRAPHIA

New visions of form, fantasy, and function

Joan Scott, editor

with the Third Coast
Computer Graphics Group

Gulf Publishing Company
Book Division
Houston, London, Paris, Tokyo

COMPUTERGRAPHIA
New Visions of Form, Fantasy and Function

Library of Congress Cataloging in Publication Data

Main entry under title:

Computergraphia: new visions of form, fantasy, and function.
   1. Computer graphics—Addresses, essays, lectures.
   2. Computer art
I. Scott, Joan E.
T385.C594 1984   001.64′43   84-8950
ISBN 0-87201-328-6

Printed in the United States of America.

Captions: Joan Scott

Book Concept and Development: William J. Lowe

Book Design: Terry J. Moore

Opposite title page: *The Mandala, a Buddhist meditation object. In oriental art, a mandala is a schematized representation of the cosmos, characterized by a concentric organization of geometric shapes. The objects here exist only as electronic impulses created with "ray tracing" techniques in a CRAY supercomputer and displayed on Evans & Sutherland Picture System. (Image conceived by Agama Publications and created by SEDIC, Inc. Tokyo.)*

CONTENTS

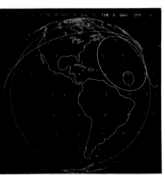
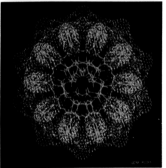
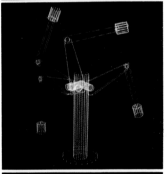

ACKNOWLEDGMENTS

On behalf of the Third Coast Computer Graphics Group, I want to express appreciation to William Lowe of Gulf Publishing Company for his extraordinary involvement in this project. He conceived the idea of an anthology presenting computer graphics as both science and art, and he worked closely with us in every phase of the book's development and production. Special thanks also to Terry Moore for his excellent page layout and cover design.

We are grateful to all the companies and individuals who together submitted more than a thousand images for our consideration. Their profuse response to our call for submissions overwhelmed and inspired us.

As editor, I want to call attention to the six contributing authors, all members of the Third Coast Computer Graphics Group, who, in addition to writing the book's text, assisted me in compiling pictures. Many other members helped with the project in essential ways. They are: Bill Bavinger, Ted Beckham, Betty Bollinger, Beverly Fitzwater, Mike Holthouse, Leo Peters, Steven Peters, Larry Purcell, Pat Schrader, Pam Schuster, Joyce Staffel, Maurice Sumner, George Tallman, and John Young.

Finally, all of us wish to acknowledge Greg Passmore, founder of Third Coast, who brought us together through his enthusiasm for the future of computer graphics.

Joan Scott

FOREWORD

From computer graphics' earliest moments, a "dim and distant" twenty or so years ago, the generation of even the simplest images by a computer has sparked a unique and compelling fascination in the human eye and mind.

In its brief history computer graphics has proven to be a remarkably successful technology. We usually define this success with catchwords like "productivity" since, after all, the technology arose from the need to perform redundant and time-consuming tasks at ultra-fast electronic speeds rather than at human rates. Early successes in applying computers to the task of generating images were usually measured in terms of beneficial productivity ratios, and today we cost-justify computer graphics in like terms.

But the real gift of computer graphics goes well beyond its labor-saving merits. And it delivers much more than just information packaged in more visually efficient bundles. There is a magic in computer graphics, a linkage between man and machine that has few parallels.

Whether the image is the design of a trivial mechanical gadget or a pseudo-colored satellite image of a desert landscape, whether a graphic design of a business logo or an intricate printed circuit board, there is beauty and art as well as the practical essence, or truth, of the information being communicated. We know that creativity is not inherent in the computer; we know further that the most sophisticated machine will not create for its user an artist talent where none existed before. But there is a fundamental beauty in computer graphics, and even years from now when it is so commonplace that we take it for granted, our lives will be enriched enormously for having been touched by it.

Randall L. Stickrod
Publisher/Editor-in-Chief, *Computer Graphics World*

COMPUTER GRAPHICS
A Technological Perspective

Jonathan Linowes

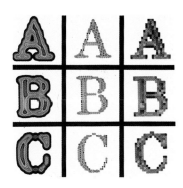

It is in our nature as human beings to build tools that extend the capabilities of our bodies and minds. We strive to design these tools to meet our needs and mold them to match our skills. Computer technology has enabled us to create tools that are more sophisticated, more powerful, and more useful than ever before. In itself the computer is simply a machine; in creative hands it becomes a companion, assistant, and communication medium. And as technology pushes beyond today's limits, *computer graphics* is often playing a leading role.

The computer is a machine that can perform millions of calculations per second. Through programming languages we can instruct the computer to manipulate not only mathematical formulas, but virtually any other type of data that can be represented symbolically. Building upon these abstract data types, we can model simulated objects and systems and manipulate them with logical procedural functions, or algorithms.

Computers communicate with the "real world" through various devices designed for the input and output of data. In the early days of computing, paper tape, punch cards, and teletypewriters were used extensively. Today, much more sophisticated techniques are employed which foster greater sensitivity of the machine to its environment and synergism with human users. As the images in this book show, computer graphics extends our eyes with new image-making ca-

Above: *A printing application shows three different raster-graphics styles. (Courtesy of Gould DeAnza and Pitney Bowes.)*

Opposite: *An untitled work by artist Joanne P. Culver.*

pabilities, our hands with interactive design tools, and our minds through non-verbal communication.

Extension of the Eye, Image-Making

"Computer graphics" is the use of computers to produce pictorial representations of information. Visual media have historically been a powerful force for expressing ideas, exploiting the natural sensitivity and perceptual response of the human visual system. Computer graphics expands the possibilities of graphic communication by combining the power of computers to rapidly store, retrieve, and process vast amounts of information with display output devices such as video screens, printers, and plotters. Integrating this technology with the more traditional fields of drafting, cartography, graphic arts, and animation provides new means for visually representing information and demonstrating relationships.

The images produced in this new medium are processed by the computer and then output to specialized display devices with graphics capabilities. In the computer the data is maintained as a structure which lends itself to the operations and analyses required by the application. Then, a sequence of display algorithms transform the data from its abstract structure into a representational image on the display device. The data models can be three-dimensional (such as architectural designs), statistical (business charts), theoretical (chemical models), or even purely conceptual (fine arts).

In creating these images, all of the principles of graphic design and visual perception come into play. The computer graphicist is an image maker and should be aware of the elements of good design, including the effective use of color, balance, layout, perspective, and other visual dynamics. It is a continuing challenge to make images that are informative, accurate, and aesthetically pleasing.

Extension of the Hand, Interaction

Beyond imaging and display, computer graphics provides the ability to interact with the data model itself. Through interaction the image becomes more than a graphic representation—it provides feedback to the user as he manipulates the model. The user is then able to interactively build, modify, and analyze the model. This feedback loop and incremental refinement is fundamental to the design process.

Solid and fragmented colors are forcefully combined in this provocative abstract. (Courtesy of James A. Squires, Chromatics, Inc.)

The input devices used for interactive computer graphics, such as the joystick, data tablet, track ball, mouse, and touch screen, transform manual actions into computer signals. The computer uses this data input to modify parameters that define a model and its image. Computer-aided design (CAD) systems have established many interaction techniques for control of the model's construction. As a design tool, constraints may be built into the system which assure the validity of the design.

The more natural it feels to use a computer, the greater its effectiveness as a design and analysis tool. Consultation with experts in particular fields is essential for developing an interactive system which responds to the users' needs and requirements. When users work more directly in the domain of their expertise, the technology itself becomes transparent.

Extension of the Mind, Spatial Thinking

Psychological and physiological studies of the past two decades have revealed evidence of two modes of human thought, ascribed to the activities of the left and right hemispheres of the brain. These cognitive modes are characterized by linguistic and symbolic functions on one side, versus non-verbal and visiospatial functions on the other. Coexisting without conflict, these two mental processes contribute to our integrated abilities to think, perceive, create, and communicate.

Left brain functions attach meaning to symbols, including words, statistics, and formulas. Traditional computer output techniques like tabular lists of numbers and printed forms utilize these mental modes almost exclusively. Computer graphics, however, as a visual and interactive medium, draws more heavily upon the spatial geometric functions of the right brain. It allows one to synthesize mental models that are manipulated as single entities, and to perceive trends and patterns in the information.

In a world traditionally dominated by the print medium and verbal expression of thought, interactive computer graphics offers a means for strengthening and more effectively utilizing the spatial cognitive modes of our brains. Users of this technology can better and more easily grasp great amounts of information, conceptualize interrelationships, and communicate ideas. All of this is made possible by recent technological advances in computer display devices, integrated circuits, and software.

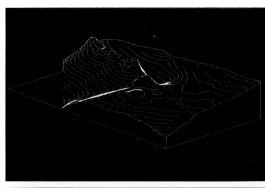

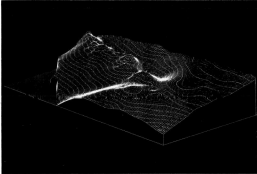

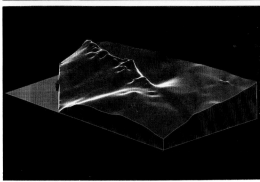

A three-dimensional subsurface geologic structure is reconstructed from seismic data in these three plots. (Courtesy of Cities Service Oil & Gas.)

Computer Graphics and Display Technologies

Computer graphics was born when someone first connected a cathode ray tube (CRT) to a computer for use as an output device. Engineers were accustomed to CRTs in the form of oscilloscopes for testing circuits and laboratory equipment. In 1950, at MIT, "Whirlwind I" became the first computer to make this connection between the computer and CRT. Advances in computer graphics technology have since been "supporting actors" to the major advances in electronics, science, and engineering, often leading the way and making greater demands.

Forming the primary basis for computer graphics display devices, CRTs have been the cornerstone of display technology. Electrons, focused into a fine beam, are projected onto a phosphorescent surface which glows when activated by the beam. The position of the electron beam and its intensity are controlled by the computer, producing a visible stroke on the screen. Eventually the glow of the phosphor decays, and the screen must be refreshed. The variety of implementations of this concept can be categorized into two classes: vector displays and raster displays.

Vector Displays

Vector CRTs are able to sweep the electron beam between any two points on the screen. The refresh tube, an early technology still in use today, has phosphors whose glow decays quickly and must be refreshed in short cyclic intervals to avoid flicker. One of the first systems employing this technology, the Evans & Sutherland Picture System I, initially designed at the University of Utah in the mid-1960s, allowed the computer or user to dynamically modify the image description data while the display device is updating the screen. This creates the effect of real-time animation, an important advantage for interactive graphics systems. However, the computing power, memory, and speed required to refresh a complex image were often prohibitive.

The direct-view storage tube (DVST) developed in the late 1960s eliminated the need for expensive memory and refresh hardware, and helped make computer graphics more affordable. DVSTs retain a stroked image on the screen for an extended time. The computer takes as long as necessary to draw a single image on these devices; and to get a new image, the screen must be erased completely. Unfortunately, this excludes the animation capability found in refresh displays.

Devices analagous to the vector CRT were developed for producing plots onto paper. These hardcopy devices move a pen across the paper, producing line drawings. Different colored pens can be used, providing the added color capability not available in the early vector CRTs.

Vector displays produce images composed primarily of lines. They are applied in fields that traditionally use this form of rendering: drafting, mechanical engineering, architectural design, electronic circuit layout, etc. Today's displays are higher-speed, and have larger memories for more complex images and color capability. (Color is limited, though, to just a few hues.) Modern design workstations often have two display screens, one for highly interactive vector graphics and another for full-color raster graphics.

Raster-Scan Displays

Raster-scan CRTs, which are much like the ordinary television tube, are emerging as the dominant display technology for computer graphics. These devices horizontally sweep an electron beam across the screen, regularly covering the entire image at a predetermined fixed rate, usually 30 times a second. The image consists of a two-dimensional matrix of dots with varying intensities. It is stored in a large memory array, or frame buffer, where each memory cell represents a single picture element (called a pixel). More sophisticated devices allow three memory cells per pixel, one each for the red, green, and blue components of a full color image.

A raster system with 256 × 210 pixel resolution and sixteen colors per image (chosen from 32,000 available shades) produced this beach scene. (Courtesy of the Hemton Group, a division of NORPAK Corp.)

A drawback of these devices is the large data bandwidth required to update a full screen, for example, more than 750,000 memory cells per frame for a full-color 512 × 512 pixel image. But the regularity of the raster refresh cycle makes the display hardware inexpensive and simple to build, utilizing technologies and standards developed for the television industry. Other major advantages of the raster-scan display include great flexibility with color, the ability to selectively modify arbitrary areas of the display down to a single pixel, and the capacity to render objects with smooth shading and realism. Most computer images, including those in this book, are produced on this type of device.

Other Display Technologies

Consider for a moment that the CRT is a tube, making it perhaps one of the most archaic components of a computer graphics system. Alternatives to the cathode ray tube have been explored, as yet without much success. These include the plasma panel and liquid crystal displays. Current research will begin to bear fruit in the near future and we can expect to see new technologies offering lightweight, high-resolution display devices.

An important part of the evolution of these display technologies is the convergence of the computer graphics, video, and photographic industries. High-resolution film recorders yield very precise, detailed photographic images. Digital video and video disc systems now are being engineered to interact with computers. Personal computers, video games, and videotext products and services all use computer graphics, bringing this exciting and sophisticated technology within the reach of the consumer. And the foundation for all of this is the exponential advances in digital hardware design.

Computer Graphics and Integrated Circuits

Until recently, the cost of hardware was a major obstacle to the growth of computer technology. Many of the early developments in computer displays were engineered to circumvent these expenses. Today, advances in computer graphics systems are being propelled by the plummeting costs of microprocessors and memory devices, due to advances in integrated circuit (IC), or chip, technologies.

Using very large-scale integration (VLSI) techniques, more than 100,000 transistors and other electronic circuit components can be contained within a single chip. Since the birth of the transistor at Bell Laboratories in 1946, the technology has evolved from small-scale integration of 1 to 10 transistors per chip, through medium-scale (100–500 transistors), to large-scale integration (1000–10,000) in the late 1970s. Meanwhile, the cost of chips has been cut at proportional rates by mass production and advanced manufacturing processes.

Chips are miniature circuits printed onto silicon in a manner similar to the commercial printing of photographs. The tiny printed circuit is then mounted into a housing, a package with protruding pins to be plugged into special computer boards. Each integrated circuit serves a particular logical function, such as memory storage, computation, or device control. A logic design engineer builds computers and other digital equipment by designing the arrangement of chips and mapping their connections to construct larger functional modules. This hardware may perform very specialized functions, or it may be designed for general ones which require

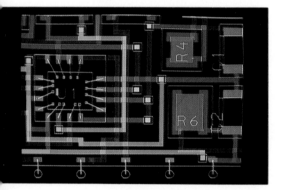

Integrated circuit design detail. (Courtesy of Applicon, a Schlumberger company.)

software programming. Computer graphics systems utilize this hardware technology in various ways for display memory, microprocessor-based workstations, and dedicated graphics processors.

Display Memory

Memory chips configured as a two-dimensional array provide dynamic storage for digital image descriptions. In vector display devices, this memory is used to store the image description as a collection of objects defined by their vector endpoint coordinates. Frame-buffer raster-scan devices, on the other hand, must have enough memory to store color values for each pixel of resolution, and this can amount to several hundred chips.

A memory chip is measured by the thousands (K) of bits of information it can store. 16K memory chips have been widely available for several years. The 64K chip, first manufactured in the early 1980s, represents a breakthrough in VLSI technology. Today 256K, 512K, and 1 megabit chips are emerging from Bell Laboratories, IBM, Japan, and other research groups, promising to deliver "double bang for the buck," and then double again.

New memory chips are currently being designed specifically for computer graphics display devices. These chips, such as the "8-by-8 display" chip developed at Carnegie-Mellon University, have features which support rapid image update and scanning.

Microprocessor-Based Workstations

Only a quarter-century ago, all computers were big machines, called mainframes. Smaller, cheaper, and slower *mini*computers were introduced in the mid-1960s. During the 1970s, yet smaller *micro*computers emerged as a hobbyist's toy, and super-minis were developed with the power of a mainframe. Mainframes themselves became faster, with incredibly high-speed "number-crunching" capabilities.

Due to advancing VLSI technologies and new system architectures, the distinctions between mainframe, minicomputer and microcomputer are dissolving and are being replaced by classifications such as personal computer, professional workstation, host, and super-computer. These new classes refer more to the machine's functional capabilities and roles than its speed, memory, and cost. Computer graphics can be found on machines of all sizes and classes.

Fisheye I, *digital fine art. (Courtesy of Zsuzsanna Molnar, Silicon Graphics.)*

The professional workstation, for instance, is rapidly evolving into an easy-to-use environment for interactive design. Computer graphics workstations are being built from general-purpose microprocessors, chips which implement most of the functions of a traditional processor. With the power of a mainframe or super-mini computer in a single chip, these workstations provide the local processing capabilities to perform complex functions accurately, to interact with the user effectively, and to rapidly display quality computer graphic images.

Workstations provide a comfortable integrated working environment for users. Computer graphics is naturally combined with other tasks, and graphical interaction techniques are employed throughout a working session, helping to make the system "user friendly." A pioneer in this area, Alan Kay, developed the first ideas for multiple windows, "mouse" interaction, and direct manipulation of objects, at the Xerox Palo Alto Research Center in the 1960s. Only recently have these capabilities become commercially available.

The explosion of interest in microcomputers, for business and personal use, is creating greater demand for advanced graphics capabilities on smaller machines. Graphics is frequently available in these products but is only beginning to approach the caliber found in professional workstations. By the end of this decade, however, high-quality computer graphics will be the norm in all personal computers, driven by high-level interactive software.

Dedicated Graphics Processors

The computer must make a vast number of computations to generate a single image. Dedicated graphics processors relieve the computer of much of these display responsibilities by performing high-level image-generation functions such as line drawing, spatial transformations, and shading of objects. These devices are specialized computers in themselves, designed for particular graphics tasks.

One type of system architecture for a graphics processor, the "pipeline," is like an assembly line of modular display functions. Data is passed from station to station, where it is mapped from one form to another. For instance, a three-dimensional model may be first positioned spatially, then mapped in perspective to two-dimensions, and finally transformed from coordinate data into pixels for display. Sophisticated graphics processors can perform these operations in

Designs dance in the darkness for this operator working with keyboard and joystick. (Courtesy of Gerber Systems Technology, Inc.)

"real time," where the update to each new image is perceived as though continuous from the last. The most advanced application of these devices has been in flight simulators for training pilots and astronauts.

Several research groups are investigating the application of VLSI technology for building dedicated graphics chips. An example is the Geometry Engine (developed at Stanford University), a chip which performs many of the pipelined display transformations. Integrating these important graphics processing functions onto a single chip will make sophisticated computer graphics available to anyone using computer services.

Pilots training in a flight simulator look out upon a computer-generated night scene on the runway. (Courtesy of Evans & Sutherland and Rediffusion Simulation.)

Computer Graphics and Software

Software drives the hardware of a computer—it tells the machine what to do. Software rarely is just "gravy" on the system; it is much of the meat itself. Hardware display devices are relatively dumb and are difficult to control. Computer graphics software packages provide libraries of programs for display and input of graphic objects, controlling color and other attributes as well as selecting the perspective for three-dimensional projections. Application programs, such as those for computer-aided architectural design or molecular modeling, use these graphics software packages for display and interaction with the user.

Software is "soft" because it is easily changed without affecting the "hard-wired" circuits of the computer and because it provides buffers (interfaces) between the various levels of system control. Imagine a hierarchical organization, with the hardware devices at the bottom level and layers of software built upon it. Each level increases in degree of abstraction, from the low-level instructions of the hardware, through the operating system which provides system utility functions, to the application programs designed to perform a user's task. As we go up through this organization we are able to instruct the machine with higher-level statements, moving away from machine-oriented tasks toward the objects and operations familiar to users in their domain of expertise—whether that be medicine, architecture, business, or art.

Computer graphics has extended the frontiers of all levels of software development. Ivan Sutherland's landmark work in 1963, Sketchpad, was the first system to develop methods for interactive graphics as a design tool for two-dimensional objects. Since then, turnkey computer graphics systems have been built and tailored to specific applications (just plug it in and "turn the key"). The development of graphics algorithms for modeling solid objects, simulating real scenes, and generating images rapidly is the subject of intense research. Standards are being defined for device-independent interfaces to graphics hardware.

Data Modeling

In the past two decades computer graphics software developments have focused, in part, on building efficient and malleable digital descriptions of spatial objects. The geometric components of a computer image, frequently organized as a hierarchy of object descriptions, must lend themselves to easy modification by application programs as well as quick rendering into graphic images.

Computer images are almost always output to a two-dimensional display medium. Using a Cartesian coordinate grid like that of ordinary graph paper, figures are specified by the X-Y coordinate endpoints, and then drawn in a "connect the dots" fashion. Enclosed areas may be filled with color or patterns. Adding a Z coordinate extends the grid into a three-dimensional space, where solid objects may be modeled and transformed. Consider the difficulty of mapping the shape of some ordinary object, say a toothbrush or a car, into this geometric coordinate description. Computer-aided design systems, like those in the automobile and aerospace industries, employ advanced methods for constructing and molding simulated objects with curved surfaces, to capture their real shapes in digital form.

Think of these models as sub-objects contained within larger objects. This structural organization allows relationships between parts of the model to be implicitly and explicitly defined. The objects themselves may be stored in coordinate form, or defined by an algorithm and generated as needed. These and other modeling techniques for graphics applications have had an impact on many other areas of software engineering.

Display Algorithms

Given some graphics hardware and a digital geometric model, how is the data transformed into a picture? This is the job of graphics display algorithms. To draw a line into a frame

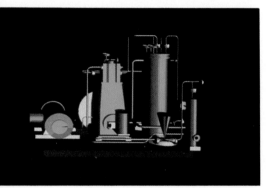

Three-dimensional, scaled model of an industrial compressor unit displayed on a color workstation. (Courtesy of Intergraph.)

buffer, the line must be converted from its natural continuous (analog) form into a sequence of discrete pixels. The line's final representation should resemble its intended form, looking like a straight line with consistent width and accurate position. The Breshenham line-drawing algorithm, for example, defines an incremental technique with minimal computation, compressing the calculation into a short arithmetic loop. Polygons (areas enclosed by a sequence of line segments) are scanned and converted into pixels for display using similar incremental techniques.

This conversion of continuous information to digital form may result in undesirable visual artifacts known as the "jaggies" or stair-stepping of lines and polygon edges on raster-scan displays. This effect is described in the Sampling Theorem, developed by C. Shannon in the 1940s at Bell Laboratories, which says that analog data must be sampled at least twice as frequently as it is changing, otherwise information is lost and impostor, or "alias," textures will appear. Techniques for reducing this effect, "anti-aliasing," use the ability to modulate the brightness of individual pixels. The visual effect of a line segment is distributed between all neighboring pixels based on their distance from the line. As a result, lines and edges look nearly continuous and may appear to have more precision than the resolution of the screen.

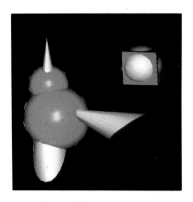

A solid modeling system can accurately represent objects piercing other objects, as demonstrated in this image rendered with shaded surfaces and simulated lighting effects. (Courtesy of Lexidata.)

The display of three-dimensional models involves additional computer graphics algorithms. To generate images with perspective, for instance, a three-dimensional object is transformed into two dimensions by mathematically projecting its geometric coordinates onto a two-dimensional plane. With perspective projection, points moving further away from the viewing position converge toward the vanishing point. (This amounts to simply dividing each X and Y coordinate by some factor of its Z distance.) Further rendering of three-dimensional objects is accomplished by additional sophisticated display algorithms.

Realistic Imaging

An object may appear to be illuminated by simulated light shining on its surface. Highlights can be added to make the object even more real-looking. Models of plastic, brass, copper, or even moon-dust can be created by varying color as a function of the spectral reflections for the particular material. Textures can be simulated on the object's surface by scattering the reflected light rays, using a predetermined pattern and perhaps a touch of randomness. Work in this area was pioneered by Jim Blinn at the University of Utah, in his quest for the "leather doughnut."

Hidden surface algorithms, for instance, determine the visible sides of three-dimensional objects modeled from polygonal tiles. To eliminate faces which intersect or overlap, the polygons are sorted by their relative X, Y, and Z coordinates and are then incrementally converted into pixels.

Another technique, ray tracing, projects rays through a modeled scene to determine the value of pixels. Originating at the viewpoint, one ray is cast for each pixel, projecting into the scene and intersecting an object at the point "visible" to the pixel. Knowing the surface angle at this point, the surface characteristics, and angle(s) of illumination, the color of the object's surface at that point can be calculated.

For shiny surfaces like metallics and mirrors, the ray continues from the reflecting surface, bouncing off other objects in the scene, making them visible in the reflection. Further, the ray may be permitted to go through a semi-transparent object, like a wine glass, and be bent (refracted) for distortions found naturally.

The composite of all the pixels on the screen, each determined by a separate ray-trace, creates a complex realistic image that may take several hours to generate, even on high-speed super-computers. These ideas have been developed by a number of computer graphics groups, including the Jet Propulsion Laboratory, New York Institute of Technology, Ohio State University, and Bell Laboratories.

Amazing recent advances in display algorithms are the products of new fields of mathematics, like "fractals" and "fuzzy sets," for displaying natural objects. Fractals are stochastic (randomly derived) models which continue to reveal texture regardless of how close you zoom up. Highly complex subjects, such as mountains and water can be modeled with very few control points and then generated with awesome realism using constrained randomness. Fuzzy sets, or the mathematics of elusive statistical probabilities, have been applied to generate images of smoke, fire, and other natural elements and phenomena.

These new techniques are opening the door to convincing computer graphic simulations that approach the natural optical quality of photographic images. There is a large market for this imagery in animation production for advertising and

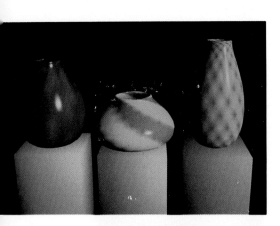

Vases on pedestals are modeled with curved three-dimensional shapes, reflective surfaces, coloration patterns, and distinct light sources. Animator: Michael Collery. (Courtesy of Cranston-Csuri Productions, Inc.)

entertainment, like that produced by visual artists at Digital Effects in New York and Lucasfilm in California.

Graphics Standards

Computer graphics is maturing as a discipline, and efforts are under way to establish standards for the industry. Device-independent graphics packages allow programs to use various computer hardware without modification. Standardization of these packages permits transporting software, models, and images between systems and simplifies adding new devices to an existing system. Standards also help hardware manufacturers address the needs of software designers.

In 1979 the Graphics Standards Planning Committee of the American organization, ACM/SIGGRAPH, released the first draft proposal of a core graphics standard for two- and three-dimensional computer graphics. Although never officially accepted, this report influenced the standards efforts which followed, including: the Programmers' Hierarchical Interface to Graphics proposal directed at three-dimensional computer-aided design applications, the Virtual Device Interface and Metafile (VDI/VDM) largely for the microcomputer industry, the North American Presentation Level Protocol System for videotext/teletext information communication services, and the Graphical Kernel System (GKS).

The GKS marks the first standard likely to be adopted by both American and European standards committees (ANSI and ISO). GKS is based on the concept of abstract graphics workstations that provide logical control of physical devices by application programs. It currently applies only to two-dimensional computer graphics, but it addresses many basic issues, including what graphical primitives ought to be available (line, polygon, text, etc.), how visual attributes are bound to objects (i.e., color and texture), plus input functions for standard interaction control. The Western and Japanese stance is to embrace this standardization with open arms, as it promises to boost productivity in the already bullish computer graphics industry.

The Future

Glimpses at the future of computer hardware in the next century can be had by looking at today's research. Integrated circuit technologies will advance from VLSI into SLSI (Super Large-Scale Integration), compacting thousands of today's ICs into a single chip. If the circuit design printed on a VLSI chip is analagous to a town or small city road map, then SLSI chips will contain the complexity of a complete road map of the entire United States! Further, chips of the future will be designed as three-dimensional lattice structures rather than two-dimensional printed circuits. They may need to be manufactured under zero-gravity in orbiting industrial space stations for economical quality control. Alternatives to silicon will be explored, such as protein-based logic circuits that may come out of new genetic bio-technology research.

These advances will lead to new digital graphic displays that provide detail resolution and chromatic response matching or surpassing that of photographic film. Computers with color graphics capabilities will be miniature enough to be truly portable, like a wristwatch or wallet. People will use them for personal and public information access, storage, and communication. Three-dimensional image displays, such as holograms, will be improved to provide realistic three-dimensional video projections for live action and computer-animated presentations.

Machine Intelligence

The future also promises "intelligent" machines, or artificial intelligence (AI), rising from the study of knowledge and decision engineering. Recent Japanese and Western commitments toward the "5th generation" of computing (the first four were tubes, transistors, LSI, and VLSI) will commercially apply AI techniques, producing intelligent machines that interact with people naturally. These machines will be easy to use, responding to our questions and instructions with informative graphics and in our own language. Computer graphic presentations will be automatically generated, showing the information we want, in the context we request.

Personal computers will evolve into intelligent assistants that can give expert advice and decision support in all areas of human endeavor, including domestic ones like cooking, home maintenance, and car repair. These assistants will be able to adapt to personal styles and respond to individual needs. Advanced symbolic processors will be required to support these programs with thousands of microprocessors working together in parallel for high-speed, high-level symbolic manipulations.

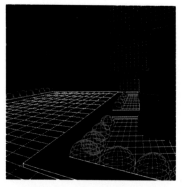

Wire City, *a fanciful design with high-tech artistic effects. (Courtesy of Digital Graphics Systems, Inc., Palo Alto, CA and Jerry Russell Blank, Blank Company, San Jose, CA.)*

Intelligent non-verbal communications between man and machine will utilize the computer graphics techniques developed today. Expert advice and problem-solving methods will be encoded and packaged into "knowledge-bases," a future commodity that will be very big business. And computer graphics will be a primary vehicle through which information and knowledge are transferred.

Information and Society

Boosted by society's technical literacy, graphic communications of the future will expand our visual literacy. Like shifting gears from the horse-drawn wagon to the automobile, the electronic visual medium is in overdrive against conventional print and publishing. These new technologies are becoming available more swiftly than were television and telephones earlier in this century. Interactive cable television, information database services, and satellite communications are feasible because of computer graphics technologies.

Nothing in the last half-century has affected our lives and the world we live in more than two inventions: the television and the computer. Computer graphics is the artful and scientific fusion of these two, and a prism refracting new visions of the earth, our lives, our inventions, our imaginations. It is the image of the future today.

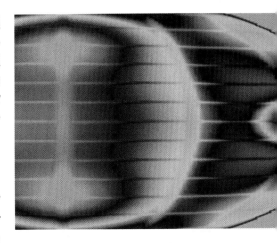

Synergy between artist and machine yielded this sensitive, organic piece called eye/OR.8. (Courtesy of J. Michael O'Rourke, New York Institute of Technology.)

1. EARTH

Richard Verm

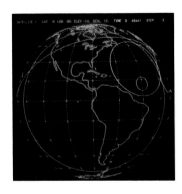

Our eyes look upon the world every day and see a few of the earth's most prominent features: its mountains, rivers, hills, oceans, trees, flowers, and wildlife. Yet, for all this vast and rich imagery, human eyes are blind to most of the planet. We can see only what is visible in sunlight; only that which is exposed at the surface. The rest of the world is visible only through manmade sensors.

These sensors can see colors beyond the range of the human eye, hear sounds too faint for the human ear. But converting the output of such devices to an understandable picture of the earth is a high challenge to human creativity and imagination.

With any measuring system there is always a degree of uncertainty about the values obtained. This uncertainty is usually labeled "noise" and quite often is just that. The source of the noise may be almost any natural phenomenon, such as an electrical storm, dust, cloud cover, or wind. Reducing the effects of noise requires a greater number of measurements, and with more and more information come the problems of data management and evaluation.

Computers and the graphic images they create have provided a whole new approach to understanding the earth. These new ideas spring directly from the computer's ability

Opposite: A close detail of a Renaissance fresco, or a subtle trick of digital imagery and pseudo-coloring? These soft contours represent the earth's surface. Mineral deposits are visualized with the aid of computer programs that suppress extraneous variation, amplify distinctions between different rock units, and aid in the discernment of intrinsic patterns. This study is based on high-resolution photography from a U-2 flight. (Courtesy of Gould DeAnza.)

to process extensive amounts of information: instead of rely-lying on a few scattered hand-processed measurements, now millions of measurements are taken and computer-processed rapidly. With more information, measurement errors become less of a factor in the interpretation. Computer graphics then provides a quick and effective means of viewing the processed data—a screen full of color-coded information can easily contain a million units of data that can be evaluated at one sitting.

Seismic Exploration

Earth scientists have been probing this planet with sound waves in search of minerals and hydrocarbons for well over half a century. Basically, the method involves bouncing sound waves off the layers in the earth's crust. A recording is made of the returning seismic waves after a disturbance (perhaps generated by an explosive charge) and plotted on paper. Initially, the interpretation of these measurements required a great deal of hand work.

Since the early 1960s the image generation has been entirely computerized. Raw data from the field is processed to remove noise and enhance the resolution of the wavefront. The processed data is then displayed on computer-controlled plotters, and from this enhanced image the geophysicist generates a map of the subsurface. Currently the emphasis in petroleum exploration is the conversion of that process from off-line hardcopy plotters to on-line interactive graphics.

The reason for the switch is two-fold. One is simply to take advantage of the computer's data management capabilities. Previously, the plotted outputs were interpreted by hand. Events of interest would be marked on the paper plot with a colored pencil. The pencil marks were transferred to a map and the surface contoured by hand. This procedure required the interpreter to spend a great deal of time simply managing paper. With a computerized display system, the data can be interpreted directly on the screen. The computer keeps track of the marks in its database. Once completed, the subsurface map can be generated and displayed automatically in a variety of modes on the screen.

A second reason for using interactive computer graphics has been the introduction of volume imaging. Instead of trying to map the subsurface by collecting a few cross sections over an area of interest, the whole subsurface is sampled as a volume. When the data in the volume is properly processed,

A contour map with colored inter-contour regions is displayed using the program GREPGS (Graphical Representation of Gridded Surfaces). (Courtesy of Dr. Anne L. Simpson, Cullen Image Processing Laboratory, University of Houston.)

a very accurate image is the result. Unfortunately, such volumes contain over a quarter-billion separate measurements. To be evaluated, the volume must be sliced into a sequence of cross sections. Producing all the cross-sectional images of interest would require hundreds of separate plots. The bookkeeping required simply to keep track of the individual plots demands computer assistance.

To aid in viewing these massive amounts of data, various types of interactive devices have been tried. The most widespread technique has been the "film loop" or animation sequence. In this method the data volume is sliced in a particular direction. The slices are arranged so that they can be displayed on the CRT in sequence much like the individual frames on a motion picture film. When viewed in this manner, the observer sees the volume slowly stripped away, revealing the structure of the interior. Variations of this approach have been developed using multiple faces of the volume. For example, the rectangular volume might be rotated so that three sides are visible. One side is then stripped away in a manner similar to the film loop technique. The difference in this approach is that instead of seeing only one face of the data volume, two or more can be seen at once.

In addition to animating through the volume, efforts have been made to look into the volume itself. Perhaps the most successful of these has been the vibrating mirror display. The display works by flexing a mirrored surface such that it sweeps an apparent volume to the viewer. As the mirror changes from concave to convex and back again the apparent focal point of the mirror's surface changes. Now when a CRT is placed above the mirror and its screen is changed in synchronization with the mirror, a three-dimensional display can be generated. This display has all the properties of a hologram—one can look from one side of an object to the other by simply moving one's head. Yet, unlike the hologram, which is a fixed static picture, the vibrating mirror display is interactive. A cursor, for instance, can be flown through its viewing volume under the control of a joystick.

Using mirror displays, the geologist or geophysicist takes several slices from the volume and displays them stacked one on top of the other. In this way the variation across several slices can be seen at once, giving the viewer a better sense of the three-dimensional relationships of the data.

Another area of computer graphics application in mineral exploration concerns the forward modeling of the seismic

Reservoir simulation uses a pie-slice representation to show underground pools of oil. (Courtesy of Cities Service Oil & Gas.)

process. Since the collection of sufficient data to map a likely prospect can be rather expensive, it is important to ensure that the field method employed will produce the intended results.

One popular approach is ray tracing. Acoustic energy travels in waves much like light or ripples in a pond. It is reflected and transmitted across boundaries in the medium of transmission. The effect of the boundaries on an acoustic wavefront can be modeled by using rays. A ray is a line always perpendicular to the wavefront and represents the path taken by an infinitesimal element of energy. The track of a ray is called a raypath.

Computing the raypath through a geological model requires a small amount of effort. The ray travels in a straight line through constant-velocity layers until it hits the interface, marking the start of the next layer. At this boundary a reflected ray and a transmitted ray are computed and each is traced to the next interface. The tracing is stopped when one of several conditions is satisfied, such as exceeding the maximum number of reflections or traveling beyond the bounds of the model.

When a set of rays is traced as a group, the wavefronts can be recreated. By generating an animated sequence on a graphics screen, the geophysicist can watch the illumination of the geologic structure with acoustic energy. From this display it is possible to evaluate the effectiveness of a seismic survey without leaving the office.

Multi-Spectrum Imaging

Remarkable advances have been made in seeing the earth beyond the spectrum available to the human eye. Satellites and high-altitude planes are the platforms for instruments that gather such pictures. From this vantage point the view can be of an entire region down to the detail of a local feature. This range in itself makes the pictures a valuable tool in mapping the earth's resources.

Landsat images from satellites orbiting the earth record the light reflected by the earth's surface across the spectrum, from infrared through the visible to the ultra-violet. By combining these different parts of the spectrum to form a single picture, "pseudo-color" pictures of the earth's surface are generated. In such images the color is not necessarily repre-

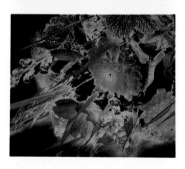

Pseudo-coloring is a software operation where one color is substituted for another through look-up tables. In the first image, flowers are displayed in normal colors. In the second and third images, pseudo-coloring has been applied. (Courtesy of Gould DeAnza.)

sentative of the objects pictured. For example, wheat fields may come out as shades of red, while bodies of water may appear black. The purpose of the coloring may be to map some changing feature of the landscape such as forest or snow cover. Sometimes colors may be chosen to highlight linear patterns in vegetation or surface topography, an indication of subsurface faulting. With careful attention the Landsat image can be used to highlight urban development, identify thermal pollution in bays or lakes, or detect surface expressions of mineral deposits.

When the Landsat data is used for mineral prospecting, an automated technique based on spectrum signatures yields a great deal of success. A spectrum signature is a count, over a portion of the picture, of the different amplitude levels in the various components of the light spectrum being returned. In application, an area known to contain the mineral of interest is outlined and analyzed. The computer then searches the whole picture for matching signatures. Wherever a match is found, that portion of the display is color-coded to indicate the degree of the match. By analyzing the clustering of signature matches, the geologist can explore a whole region which might have been previously inaccessible. In fact, this technique has been used to locate mineral deposits that had been overlooked by ground surveys.

A lake is pseudo-colored orange in this Landsat image. (Courtesy of Gould DeAnza.)

Earth imaging from satellites is not limited to Landsat and measurements of light reflectance. Radio and micro waves are being used to penetrate cloud cover, vegetation, and shallow surface debris. For example, a recent Space Shuttle mission used a radar mapping system to scan the Sahara Desert. Computer enhancement of the results revealed a network of river channels buried under the sand.

Other satellites have instruments to measure the earth's magnetic field, gravitational field, and radiation pattern. Such information is used in navigation, mineral exploration, and geodesy. Once again the analysis of this data requires computer-generated graphics.

Weather

Perhaps the application of computer graphics that most often touches our lives is in weather forecasting. Almost everyone has seen the "weather radar" or latest satellite image on the evening news report. These color pictures are all created by computer graphics systems. They represent a great improvement over the black-and-white pictures available a decade ago, yet they show only a small portion of the information that the weather forecaster accesses.

These scientists must deal with a very complex volume of data. Where the evening news simply shows intensity of rainfall using a color scale, the weather service must analyze many more factors: wind velocity and direction, temperature, cloud formation, and barometric pressure—all as a function of ground location, altitude, and time.

To get a better grasp of the problem, imagine trying to keep track of all air movements, at all altitudes, over the entire North American continent, throughout the day. This is what is required for an accurate weather forecast.

Central to the forecasting problem is that although the instrumentation to make these measurements exists, an appropriate display with the capacity to convey all the information is missing. For example, the two geostationary weather satellites (GOES EAST and GOES WEST) can scan most of North and South America in synchronization to produce three-dimensional stereo images. From the stereo pairs, cloud heights can be computed; and by frequent scanning (three-minute intervals), wind velocity and direction can be computed from adjacent images. A display of *all* the information would require a five-dimensional plot.

Attempting this level of data concentration on a two-dimensional CRT has been successful with color-coded three-dimensional stereo images that are viewed with special glasses. The three-dimensional effect of the stereo images gives the altitude information, while arrows show wind direction and velocity. Such a display is only useful given the computational speed of computer graphics.

The Future

Current trends in the earth sciences show that computer graphics will play an ever-expanding role in our lives and our perceptions of the world. Displays with greater capacity and resolution will be required to evaluate the accumulated volumes of data, and graphic displays in three-dimensional space will become ever more necessary as multiple data types and volumes must be investigated simultaneously. It is all part of a changing, expanding view of our earth.

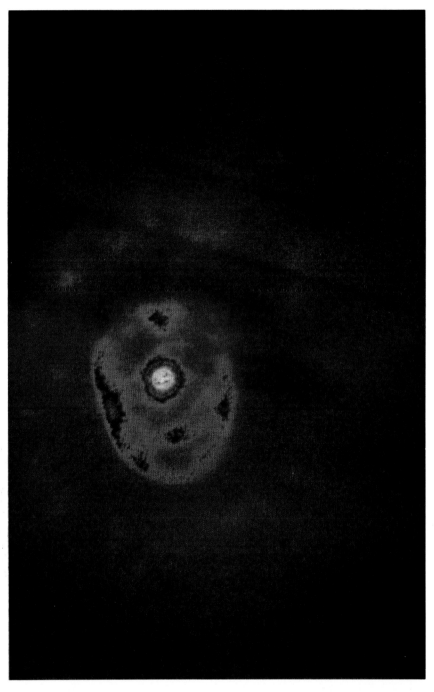

A telescope gathered physical data from a distant galaxy, a computer image processing system refined the data, enhanced it with color imaging, and a team of astronomers was rewarded with this stunning sight. (Courtesy of the Institute for Astronomy—University of Hawaii and Gould DeAnza.)

When storm clouds gather, forecasters watch the sky from high above the earth. The GOES-WEST weather satellite transmits pictures as digital data to a ground station, where the pictures are reconstructed and enhanced through computer image-processing techniques. Pseudo-coloring translates gray days and black clouds into bright hues to indicate atmospheric conditions. (Courtesy of MacDonald Dettwiler and Gould DeAnza.)

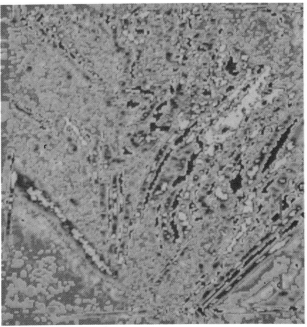

Probing deep underground, geologists seek hidden oil reservoirs. A grid of sensitive instruments on the surface of the earth detects shock waves which are created by strategically placed explosive charges and are reflected by subsurface structures. The seismic data these instruments collect is then processed with the aid of computer graphics. These color plots of acoustic reflection amplitudes are a vertical slice **(top)** and a horizontal slice **(bottom)** through a model of an oil field in the North Sea. A geologist working with these two plots can visualize the three-dimensional formations below the earth. (Courtesy of Dave Fisher, Bill Smith, and Richard Verm, Cullen Image Processing Laboratory, University of Houston.)

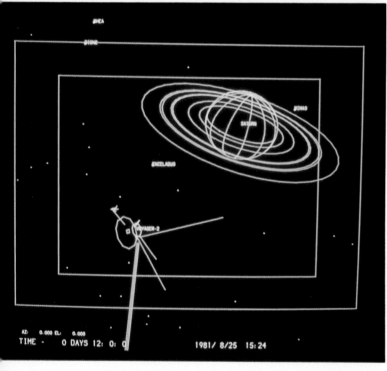

Cartoons serve a scientific purpose in this computer-animated sequence (top) selected from a film showing the Voyager I spacecraft passing the planet Saturn. Each frame in the fly-by animation sequence was created from a matching frame in the skeletal storyboard (bottom). Computer calculations based on the laws of dynamics controlled the simulated movement of the objects, while textured surface generation techniques and computations derived from the laws of optics generated the realistic models, complete with shadows. (Courtesy of the Jet Propulsion Laboratory and Gould DeAnza.)

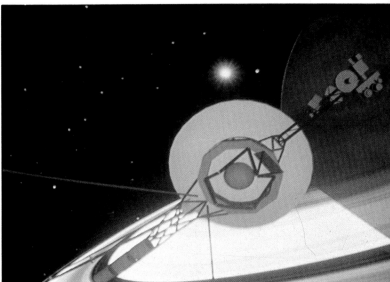

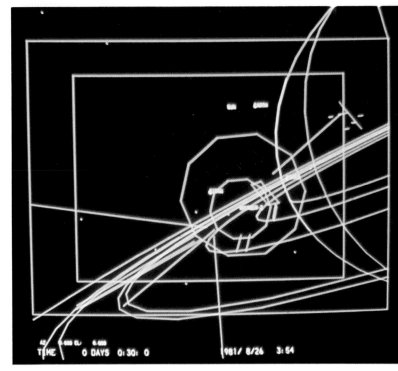

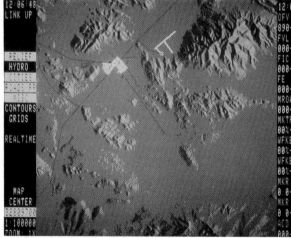
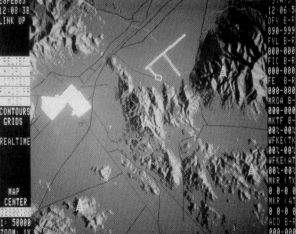

Resembling a western landscape painting, the top image is actually a ground-level view from an interactive terrain map used for battle simulation exercises. The two displays above are aerial views of the same terrain. Objects below become larger and more detailed as the viewer approaches the ground. Computer control commands appear on both sides of the screen. This computer-generated imagery can be run as an animation for pilots learning to fly over the area. (Courtesy of Science Applications, Inc. and Gould DeAnza.)

The southwest portion of Mount Rainier, looking northeast toward the mountain. This scene was generated by computer from Defense Mapping Agency data, with a "pseudo terrain" composed between the actual known data points and the elevations. A fractal algorithm was employed to generate a more realistic model of the natural terrain. (Courtesy of Boeing Aerospace Company.)

An Air-Launched Cruise Missile flies low over the terrain in this scene created entirely by computer. In the future, a fighter pilot may have an alternative to looking out the cockpit window or relying on radar, which the enemy might detect. Instead, he may look at a screen displaying a movie of the terrain ahead, constantly updated from information stored in the computer database and from sensors in the aircraft. (Courtesy of Boeing Aerospace Company.)

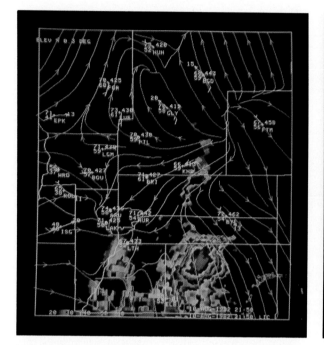 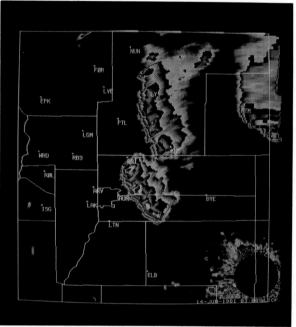

Through a network of weather-reporting stations, Colorado meteorologists gather data on temperature, dewpoint, wind speed and direction, pressure visibility, solar radiation, and precipitation every five minutes. A computer-processed image of the data allows rapid, precise local forecasting. **Left:** Winds carrying moist air (blue lines) are converging near Denver (outlined by LAK, ARV, and AUR), indicating the likelihood of thunderstorm development in the area within an hour. The storms are right on time **(right),** arriving just outside Denver 30 minutes later. Colors indicate the intensity of precipitation. (Courtesy of the National Oceanic and Atmospheric Administration, PROFS Program, Boulder.)

Opposite: The vibrant colors in this geographic tapestry represent surface features: water, trees, grass. The patterns are derived by computer graphics methods using remote sensing imagery transmitted from an earth-orbiting satellite. Close examination reveals a multitude of tiny squares, the individual pixels. A computer can tabulate the number of pixels of each color to provide a summary of the acreage covered by each vegetation type. (Courtesy of NASA-Ames Research and Gould DeAnza.)

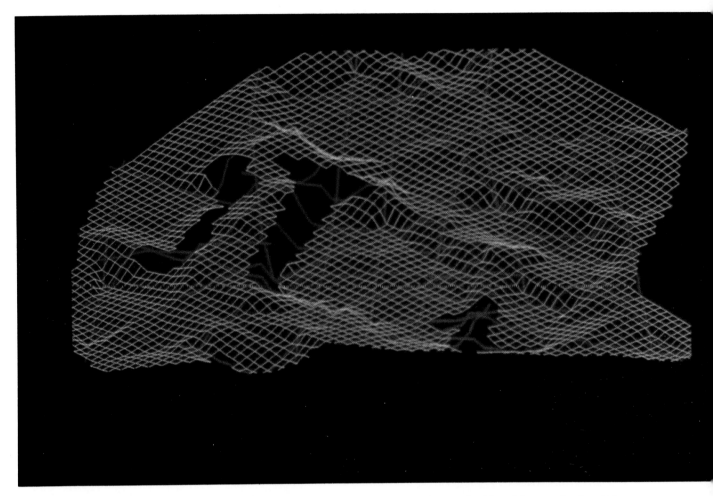

Like a bright orange net cast over invisible points, this computer-generated mesh outlines the surface contours of an unseen underground geological formation. The red lines are the results of a seismic survey. Instead of intuition, today's wildcatter relies on three-dimensional models like this in deciding where to drill for oil. (Courtesy of Intergraph.)

Opposite: In the same way a biologist applies stains to a tissue sample for viewing under a microscope, the astronomer applies pseudo-color to telescopic photographs to differentiate galactic components. (Courtesy of Institute for Astronomy, University of Hawaii and Gould DeAnza.)

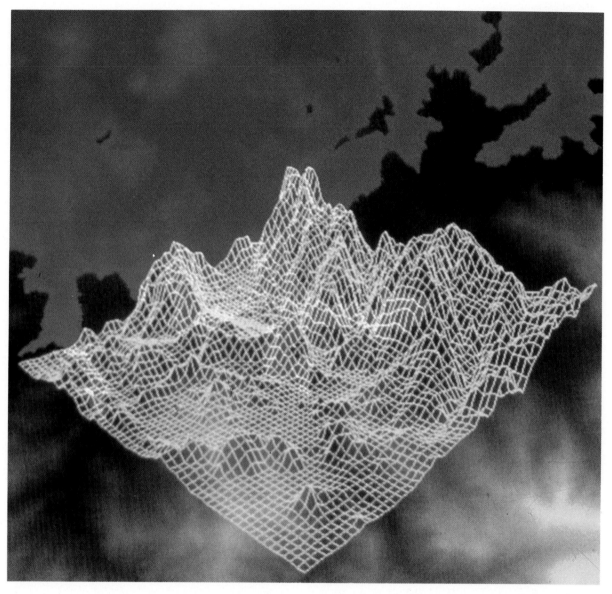

The hazy blue and brown image in the background is an unenhanced Landsat photograph. Data derived from this original is processed mathematically to generate the white and yellow mesh which distinguishes the topographical features of the surface. (Courtesy of Gould DeAnza.)

Opposite: Beauty is deceiving. This striking picture shows an ecological disaster. It is a Landsat photograph of Kentucky coal fields, pseudo-colored by computer to show areas destroyed by strip mining. A color is assigned to each of the four standard spectral bands utilized by Landsat satellites: three in visible light, one in infra-red. Rock and soil composition are determined by the way light reflects off surface features. (Courtesy of Environmental Research Institute and Gould DeAnza.)

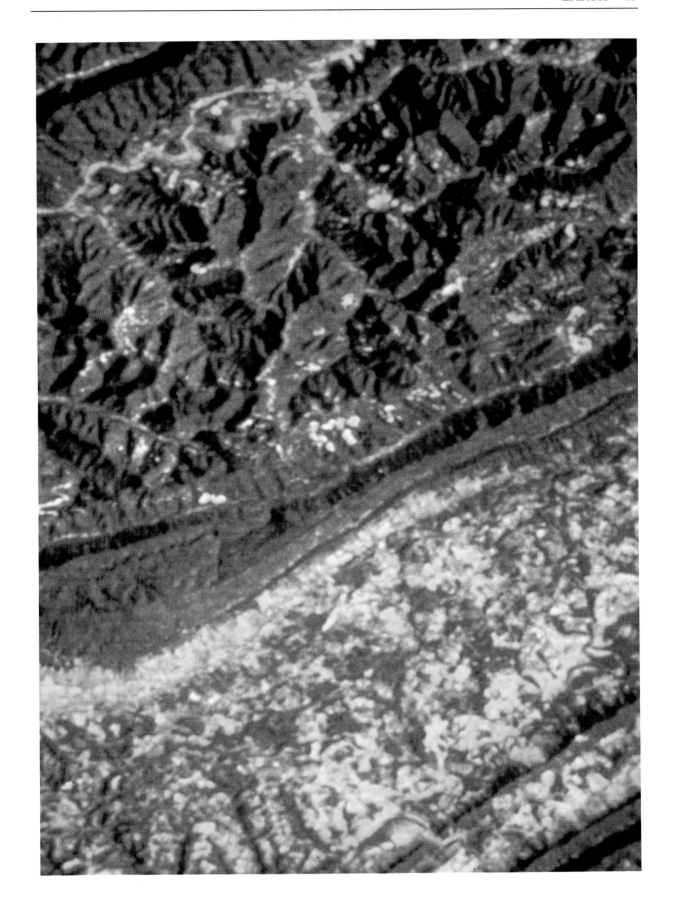

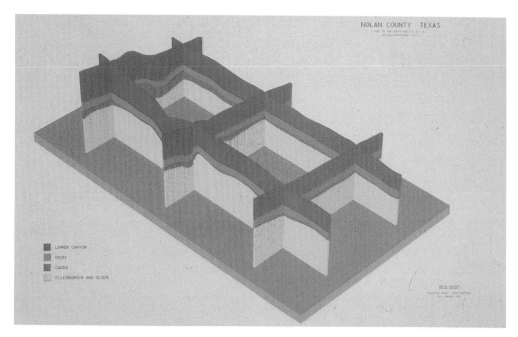

What would judges at a Science Fair think of this stand-up cardboard model of underground geological formations? In fact, this model exists only in digital (numerical) form inside the computer—the picture was produced with an ink jet plotter. For obvious reasons, this method of presenting seismic data is called a "pseudo fence diagram." Each intersection of the fence corresponds to a seismic test point. The vertical plane is a cross section into the earth. (Courtesy of R. G. Graf, Cities Service Oil and Gas.)

A geological fault line runs between the red and green in this three-dimensional display of a structure within the earth's crust. Though these delicate colors produced by an ink jet plotter are much prettier than the rocks they represent, it is the clarity of data presentation, not cosmetics, that justifies the use of computer graphics in petroleum exploration. (Courtesy of R. G. Graf, Cities Service Oil and Gas.)

In the beginning, God created the heavens. Ever since, mankind has been fascinated by their mysteries. The magnificent galaxy Centaurus A, thirteen million light years away, is dramatically colored through computer image enhancement to show "isophotes" (lines of constant brightness). By studying isophotes astronomers can create mathematical models of objects. (Courtesy of European Southern Observatory and Gould DeAnza.)

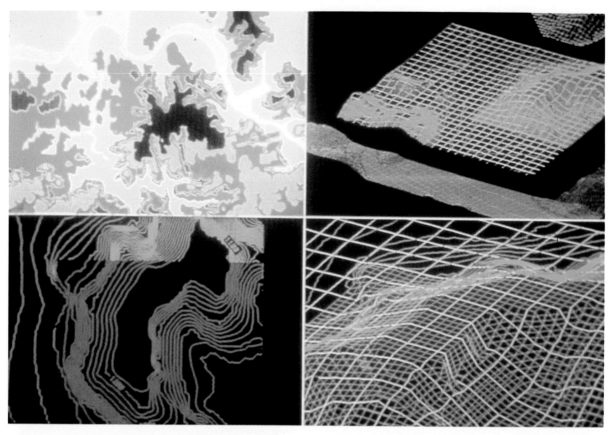

A matter of perspective: In science, as in art, there are many ways to look and to see. Here, four different representations of a terrain model, displayed together on a graphics work station, help the geologist visualize field formations. **Top left:** A color-coded map. **Top right:** Overview of a three-dimensional topological mesh. **Bottom right:** Close-up of the highest peaks in the mesh. **Bottom left:** A contour plot, where each line traces a path of constant elevation or constant depth. (Courtesy of Intergraph.)

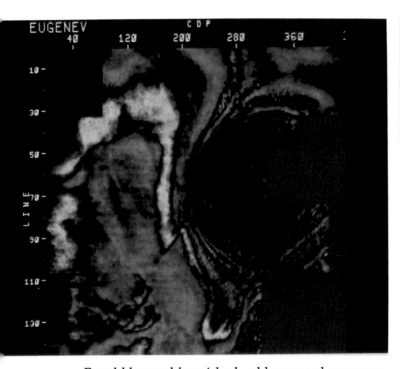

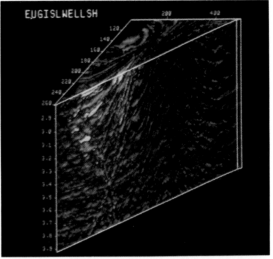

Royal blue and burnished gold seem colors appropriate to the finding of oil and the wealth it means. These images are taken from a U.S. government demonstration of three-dimensional processing of seismic data to find oil. The large picture shows the underground tract from a simulated overhead viewpoint. The three smaller pictures are examples of data cut in three dimensions for analysis. Computer graphics has been used to superimpose a geometric outline and numeric calibrations. In each figure the vertical line represents depth into the earth and the numbers on the vertical axis indicate timings. The top plane is parallel to the earth's surface; the numbers are location codes. (Courtesy of Gould DeAnza.)

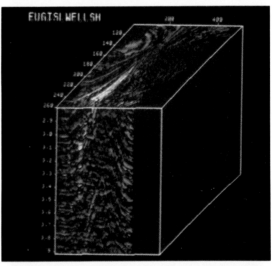

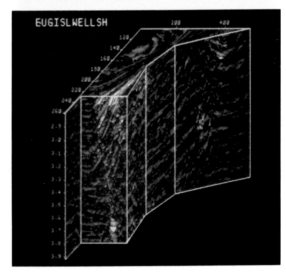

Mathematical landscapes unfold through digital merging of topographic data with Landsat data. The mosaic-like quality of the image occurs because square arrays of pixels have been assigned the same color, that color being calculated from all relevant individual pixels. This technique emphasizes major characteristics of a geological surface while suppressing more subtle differences. (Courtesy Iris International and Digital Graphic Systems, Inc.)

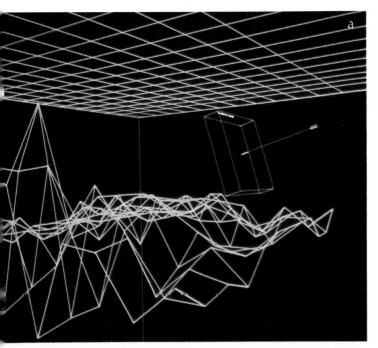

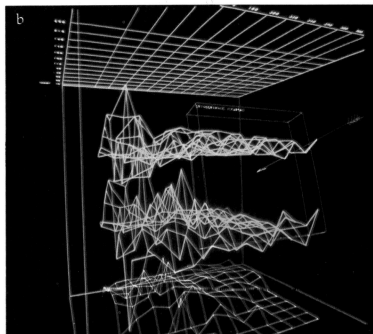

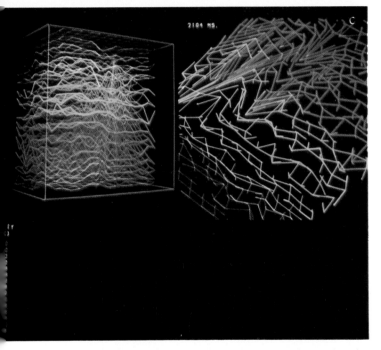

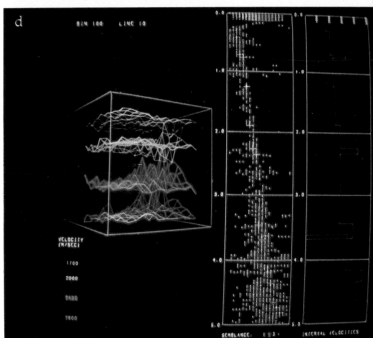

Like apparitions in a darkened room during a séance, these neon-bright seismic velocity models were conjured from the computer to help geologists organize and interpret their data. **(a)** A close look at a single velocity surface. The red hat box with arrow is a slicing apparatus which can be manipulated to any shape, location, and orientation. **(b)** Three velocity surfaces are displayed.

The peak in the green surface corresponds to a salt dome. **(c)** Separate colors represent 16 velocity surfaces, displayed on the right. On the left is the slice, the contents of the red hat box. **(d)** The four velocity surfaces in the middle of the picture can be interactively modified in real time. (Courtesy of Evans & Sutherland and Geosource, Inc. Programmed by Ivan K. Scheffler.)

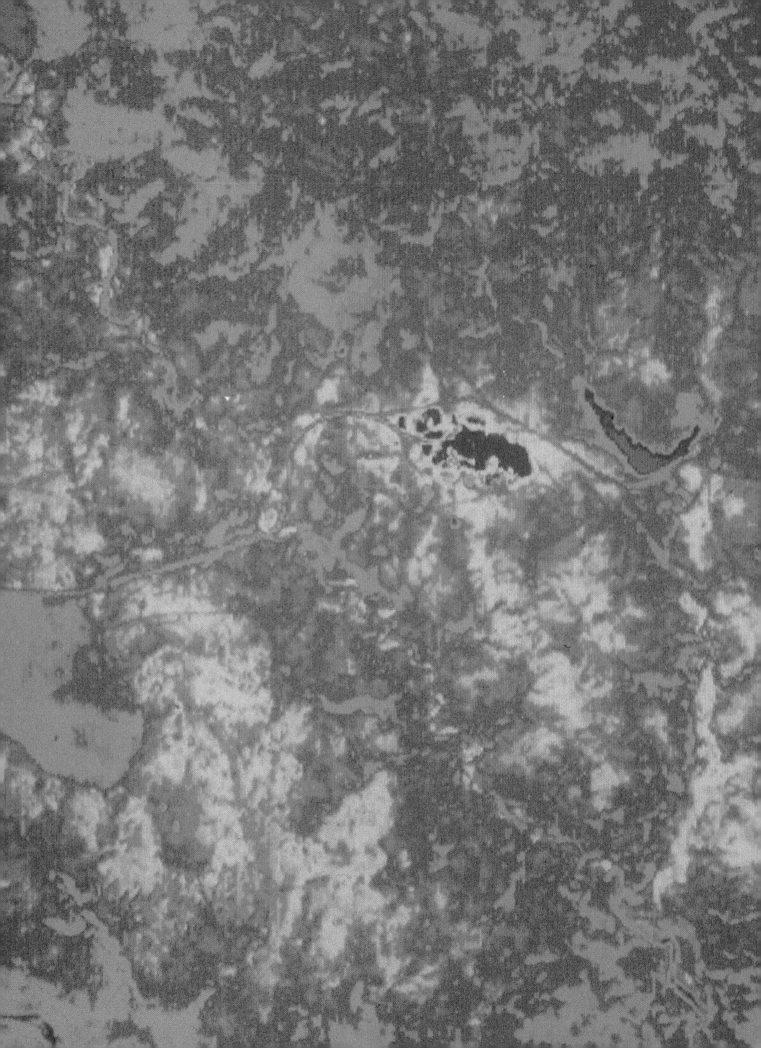

Though it might look like the moon, this is Crater Lake in Oregon. The crater is shown here in a digitally enhanced photograph, produced using technology akin to that which brings pictures back from the moon. The raster-format data is an array of pixels, 1,000 by 1,000 in resolution, or four times sharper than a home television picture. (Courtesy of NASA-Ames Research and Gould DeAnza.)

Opposite: Hot spots on cool backgrounds, these underground coal fires jump out as a result of artful pseudo-coloring of Landsat images. Satellite photographs of areas of the earth's surface are enhanced by a computer scientist's judicious choice of colors to represent values present but not obvious in the original image. (Courtesy of Gould DeAnza.)

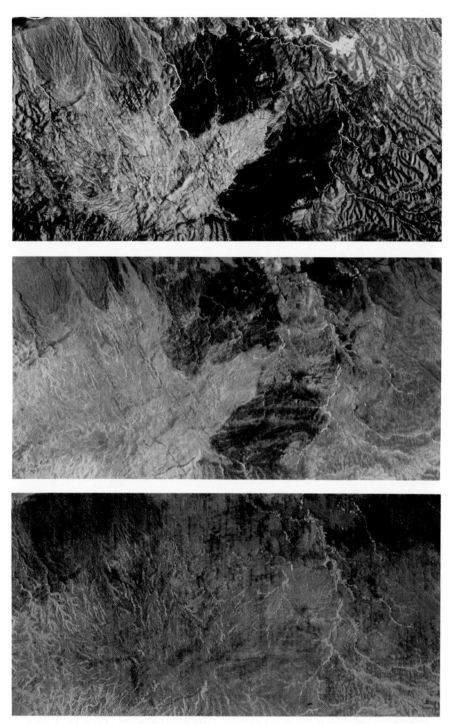

Delicate, dreamy watercolors tint the surface of the parchment as scientists play with permutations beyond the reach of painters. Remote sensing images taken at selected wavelengths comprise a database that has been manipulated by alternate enhancement procedures. The objective is to identify deposits of minerals with differing spectral signatures in the land area surrounding an Arizona silver mine. (Courtesy of NASA-Ames Research and Gould DeAnza.)

The vast Pacific Ocean captured in a single glimpse, the turbulence of the upper atmosphere revealed, the dominant air currents charted, all thanks to the GOES-WEST weather satellite and computer graphics. (Courtesy of MacDonald Dettwiler and Gould DeAnza.)

The Potomac River's veins infiltrate Washington, D.C., and the massive, sprawling government buildings are obscured by the natural features of the surface in this Landsat image. This is one "source document" for the huge geographic databases that help monitor our nation's environment. (Courtesy of Optronics International, Inc.)

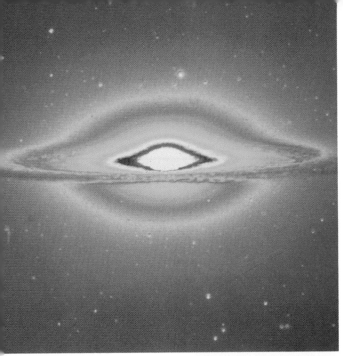

Like a chameleon changing the color of its skin, the Sombrero galaxy presents three different appearances. Astronomers study the galaxy using pseudo-coloring for image enhancement to reveal different components **(top)** and isophotes **(middle).** An edge detector algorithm was applied to generate the bottom view. (Courtesy of Gould De Anza.)

In this satellite's-eye-view of San Francisco Bay, the Golden Gate Bridge really is golden, and so are the San Mateo and the San Francisco-Oakland Bay bridges—thin gold lines across the bright green bay. The solid blue at the lower left is the Pacific Ocean. The color selection reveals a human touch, because the computer would just as soon apply pink to the values that identify the surface of the ocean in this Landsat photograph. (Courtesy of Gould DeAnza.)

Tambora, a volcano in Indonesia, has a conspicuous crater surrounded by ash deposits (brown). Vegetation (pink and red) covers portions of its slopes; other parts are covered by solidified lava flows (shades of blue). These colors were applied by a classification program, where the objective is the identification of all pixels that have the same image characteristics. A control set of pixels defines the characteristics sought, the computer then tabulates all relevant pixels and pseudo-colors those falling into a particular classification. (Courtesy of the Lunar and Planetary Institute, Houston, and Gould DeAnza.)

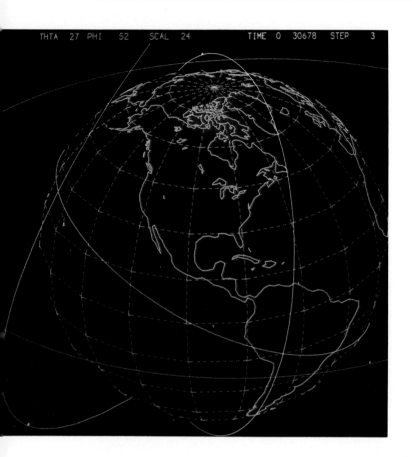

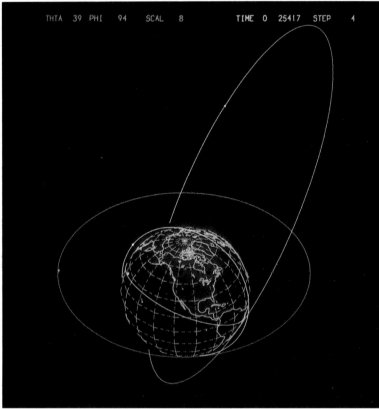

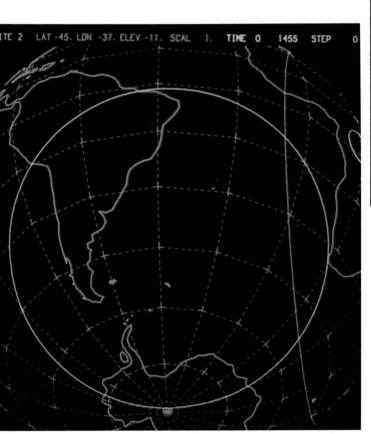

Satellites leave tracks, but it takes computer graphics to find them. A real-time, interactive, animated astrodynamics simulation of the earth with several satellites and their orbits provided these four excerpts. (Courtesy of Peter W. Baker and Victor H. Leonard, Boeing Aerospace Company, and Evans & Sutherland.)

a

b

A faint signal is transmitted across empty space from a tiny space craft, received by an antenna on earth, and passed to waiting computers for processing. The result: close-up views of Saturn, its rings, and its moons. **(a)** Montage of Saturnian moons with Dione front, Tethys and Mimas right, Enceladus and Rhea left, and Titan distant top. **(b)** Color-enhanced image of the planet. **(c)** Saturn and rings from a range of 1.5 million kilometers. **(d)** A pseudo-color image of a ring showing areas of different chemical composition. The first three views were transmitted from Voyager I; the last, from Voyager II. (Courtesy of Jet Propulsion Laboratory.)

c

d

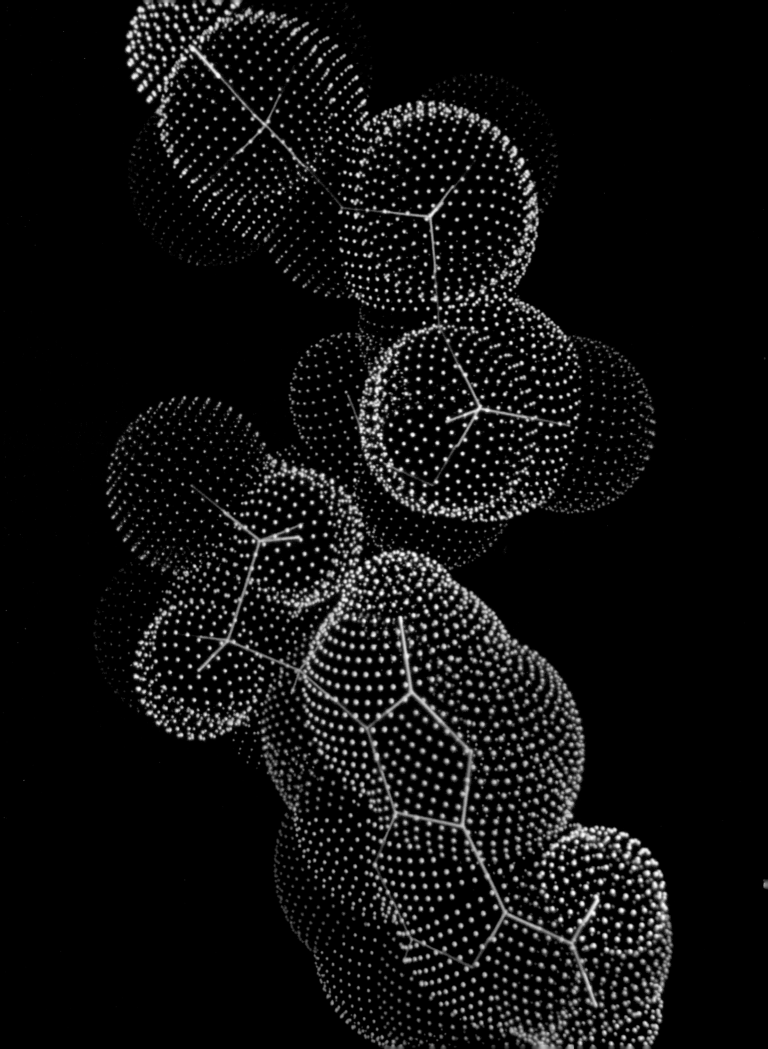

2. LIFE

Allen Buford

Computer graphics as a tool for physicians is certainly one of the most exciting and challenging advances in modern medicine. Since x-rays were discovered by Wilhelm Roentgen in 1895, scientists have sought to provide sharper and more detailed views of the human anatomy for diagnostic and theraputic evaluation. Modern techniques such as computerized tomography (CT), emission computed tomography (ECT) or nuclear medicine, nuclear magnetic resonance (NMR), and positron emission tomography (PET) have greatly reduced the need for surgery in many cases and have provided invaluable information about the physiology of the human body. Most hospitals now have CT scanners and over half of all general hospitals with more than a hundred beds have nuclear medicine facilities.

Computerized tomography uses an array of x-ray generators which move around the patient. An image processing computer collects the data and then reconstructs a three-dimensional display of the desired area to be studied. Using the computer, a physician may reconstruct different views of

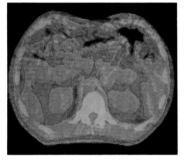

Computerized axial tomography of the abdomen of an adult. (Courtesy of the Department of Radiology, St. Luke's Episcopal and Texas Children's Hospitals and the Texas Heart Institute, Houston.)

Opposite: *Molecular structure of adenosine triphosphate (ATP), the body's primary energy-storage molecule. The simplest drawings of molecules have a line segment for each bond. But, to understand the interaction of enzymes, hormones, and drugs within the body, it is necessary to know the location of the molecular surface. Computer drawings are an important tool in analyzing the three-dimensional structure of molecules. Illustrated here is a rapid method for generating an image of the molecular surface. The MIDAS computer program scatters dots across the surface at an approximately constant density per unit area. The line drawings inside are the covalent chemical bonds. (Courtesy of Evans & Sutherland and The Computer Graphics Laboratory, University of California, San Francisco. © Regents of the University of California.)*

any portion of the patient's body which was scanned. This offers the physician the opportunity to see other views when an abnormality is found, without taking additional x-rays. The computer can also be directed to change the contrast of the image to highlight selected details.

Nuclear medicine involves the use of radioactive isotopes as a source for producing images. These isotopes first became available after World War II and the medical community responded quickly with the introduction of the rectilinear scanner in the 1950s. Images are produced by first injecting the patient with one of several different isotopes. Next, the scanner produces images of internal organs by scanning the patient and giving a count of the radiation at each point scanned. These counts are then displayed as gray-scale or colored dots giving a three-dimensional view of the selected site.

Improving on this method, the scintillation camera was introduced in the 1960s. This camera allows scanning an entire image in a single instant rather than line-by-line as with the rectilinear scanners. The scintillation camera, or gamma camera, also provides the ability to make several successive images. These images can then be viewed in a continuous loop mode to provide an animated view of the organs being studied. The development of this tool meant that for the first time in the history of medicine a physician could study organs at work without surgery. Similarly, travel of fluids through the body can be watched as a means of detecting blockages or ruptures.

An international spirit of cooperation has been one of the necessary elements for the effective use of computers in medicine. Advancements in machines and instruments have contributed greatly, but without programs and methods of manipulating the gathered data, much of the usefulness of these modern devices would be lost. Development of algorithms and computer programs has been a worldwide effort, and the interface of this knowledge with the machines has allowed computer graphics to become an integral part of the modern hospital.

Computerized tomography has its roots in work done by an Austrian mathematician, J. Randon. His work demonstrated that a slice of a three-dimensional object can be created if a set of all of its projections is known. Computerized tomography and nuclear medicine use computers to generate these image slices from data acquired through x-rays and radioactive isotopes. Newer techniques such as nu-

Positron emission tomography (PET) scan of a rabbit heart with pseudo-color assigned to the originally monochrome image by means of a "white heat" table. (Courtesy of Comtal/3M, Altadena, California.)

clear magnetic resonance use radio frequencies or magnetic pulses to generate the three-dimensional data.

The first published NMR images were produced by Paul C. Lauterbur of the State University of New York in 1973. Advanced displays using Fourier-transformation imaging were then demonstrated by A. Kumar, D. Welti, and R. R. Ernst of the Swiss Federal Institute of Technology in 1975. Nuclear magnetic resonance uses this as one method of producing images from the acquired data. Another method, which uses oscillating magnetic fields to select planes, was devised by Waldo S. Hinshaw of the University of Nottingham.

Computer-based imaging techniques are in widespread use as aids both in diagnosis and treatment. Nuclear cardiology can diagnose improper heart function and identify damage done to the heart from strokes or heart attacks. Flow of blood through arteries can also be checked by tagging blood cells and watching their flow through the circulatory system. These non-invasive methods often can be used as an alternative to surgery.

Nuclear medicine is used to detect abnormalities in the brain; neurosurgeons also employ computerized tomography as a guide, before and during operations. Nuclear medicine is further used to study organs for correct size and function as well as to verify results of surgery or transplants. For example, after kidney transplants, radioactive fluids trace the flow through the new kidney to verify its ability to function.

Finally, computerized tomography imaging is being used to diagnose and treat various forms of cancer. CT images are used to locate lesions and aid in determining dosages in radiation therapy. The ability of computerized tomography to view the body in three dimensions allows physicians to better determine the size and mass of the lesions. As physicians become more familiar with these technologies and as equipment becomes more available, additional uses of nuclear medicine will be found.

When the double-helix structure of DNA was discovered in 1953, a model was made using wire and metal plates soldered together. Today, chemists and biologists are using computers and cathode ray tubes (CRTs) to display three-dimensional models of molecules. Ball-and-stick models which resemble tinker toys are still used to a great extent, but as costs of equipment drop and turnkey systems are produced, more laboratories are using computer graphics as a research tool for molecular modeling.

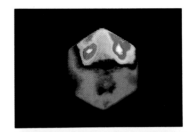

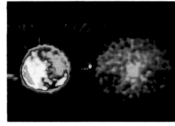

These cross sections of the abdomen are images generated through emission-computer tomography (ECT). The first patient (top) has two normal kidneys. The second patient has received a renal transplant, and the image shows that the new kidney is functioning well. (Courtesy of The Department of Radiology, Hermann Hospital, Houston.)

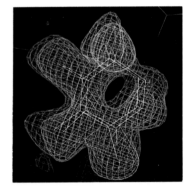

Models of a sugar-binding protein are fitted to contoured electron density cages in a study of how living cells get nutrients. (Courtesy of Evans & Sutherland and Rice University.)

There are many methods for creating and viewing these models, depending upon the form of the display to be used. Output may be on a pen plotter, on a raster CRT, or on a vector CRT. One such program is PLT1, which uses concentric multicolored circles on a plotter to represent molecules. Another program, called PLUTO, adds hatching to simulate a light source. Hidden-line drawings of ball-and-stick type models can be produced by Ortep-II. Another package called Chemgraf uses overlapping circles of different intensities to give the illusion of highlights and shadows.

The latest efforts include interactive viewing of molecules. In these systems, such as those by Michael Pique and Nelson Max, a user can manipulate a cursor to rotate the model and look at various views on a raster CRT. Other systems such as GRAMPS and FRODO focus on the input of the model either from a sketch made on the terminal or by accessing molecular structures from a database.

As the science of holography (three-dimensional image projection) advances, physicians and researchers hope that a link with computer graphics will greatly enhance their ability to study these models.

Using such techniques, scientists are better able to understand relationships between molecules and to study some of the forces involved in such activities as crystal growth and chemical bonding. Pharmaceutical companies are using computer graphics to model new compounds for their ability to bind with other molecules. With this information they hope to make drugs which have greater efficacy and fewer side effects. Similarly, on a larger scale, work is being done in simulation of cell activity. Replication of cells can be simulated graphically to view growth and determine effects of outside agents on cell cultures. Imaginative biologists speculate that one day we may be able to simulate cell reproduction in the human body in such a manner as to be able to watch the process of division from a single cell to a fully developed embryo.

Computer graphics has permanently changed the way we live. Directly or indirectly we are all affected by computer graphics almost daily. If we become seriously ill, chances are almost certain that computer graphics will play a part in our treatment, and probably a major one. Advances in cellular biology and chemistry through the use of graphics provide us with a better understanding of the basic life processes and the promise of a better and healthier future.

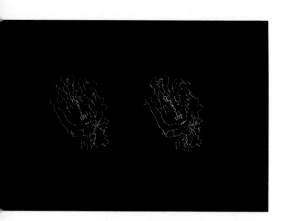

Selective representation of carbon atoms in an enzyme molecule. The images are not quite identical—they form a "stereo pair" (see page 58, top). (Courtesy of R. K. Wierenga, State University Groningen, The Netherlands.)

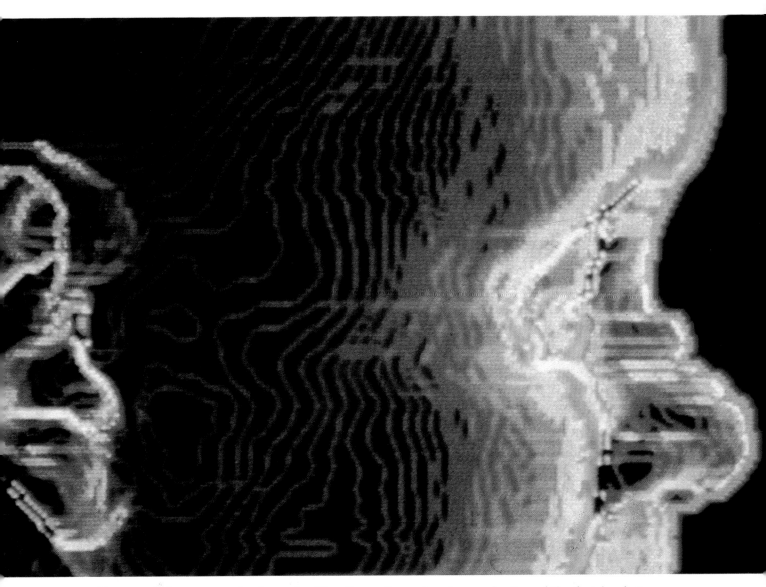

Reconstructive surgery is planned with a three-dimensional reproduction of the facial soft tissue and the skull, created from computer tomography scans. (Courtesy of Mallinckrodt Institute, Washington University School of Medicine, St. Louis, and Gould DeAnza.)

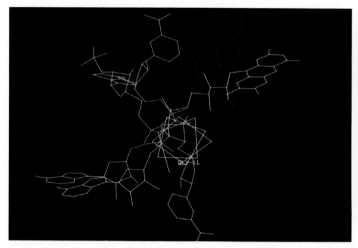

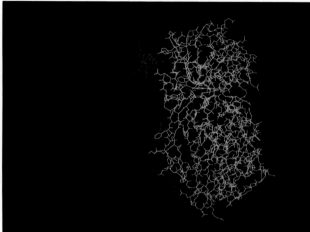

Left: Research on the structure and function of enzymes produced this picture to illustrate the similarity in binding of four nucleotides when the phosphate-binding helixes are superimposed.
Right: Lively colors were created by photographing a black-and-white screen using different color filters. Here the positions of approximately 3,000 atoms in the enzyme-substrate complex of p-hydroxybensoate hydroxylase are shown. The flavine and the substrate are indicated in yellow. The polypeptide chain, composed of about 393 amino acids, is folded into three units, as indicated with green, blue, and red. (Courtesy of Evans & Sutherland and the State University Groningen, The Netherlands.)

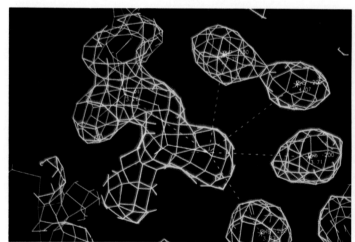

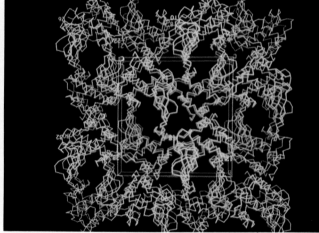

Left: A sample of a substance with unknown molecular structure is tested, and its electron density distribution is reconstructed from x-ray diffraction data. The data is contoured in three perpendicular planes, which gives a cage-like wire mesh surface (blue) where the interpolated density takes on a specific value. The proposed computer model is made out of vector sticks (pink), which are interactively manipulated.
Right: Electric-green discharges seem to jump out of this lively abstract. The image was created to study the crystal structure of the protein lysozyme. The green lines are the simplified structure of several adjacent molecules. The violet outline of a cube in the center defines a unit cell, the smallest volume that can contain components equivalent to a whole molecule. (Courtesy of Evans & Sutherland and the Laboratory of Molecular Biophysics, Oxford University.)

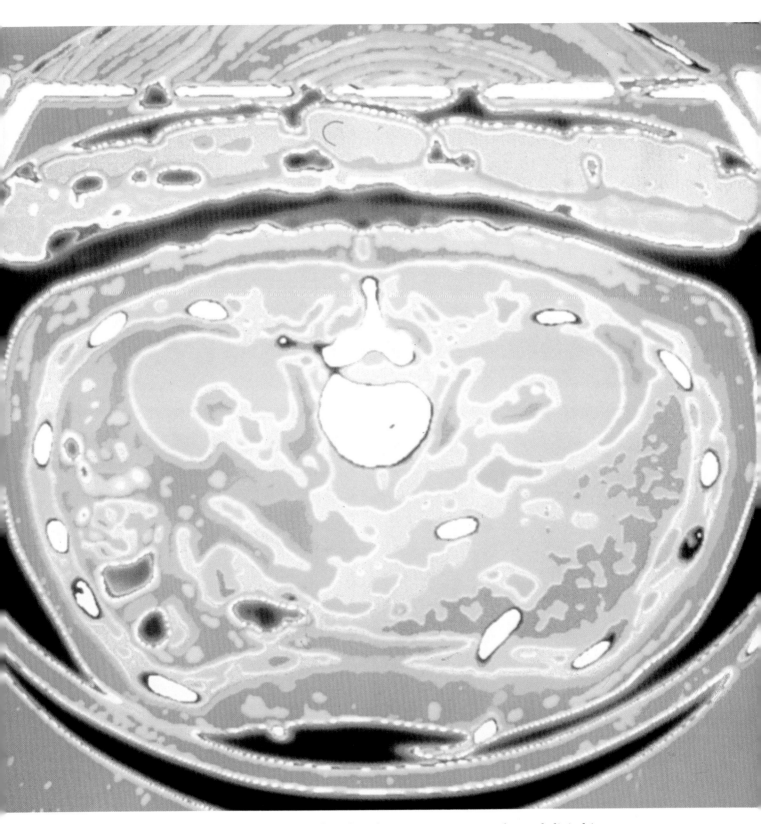

A colorful representation of a kidney produced with computer tomography and digital image enhancement techniques. (Courtesy of Gould DeAnza.)

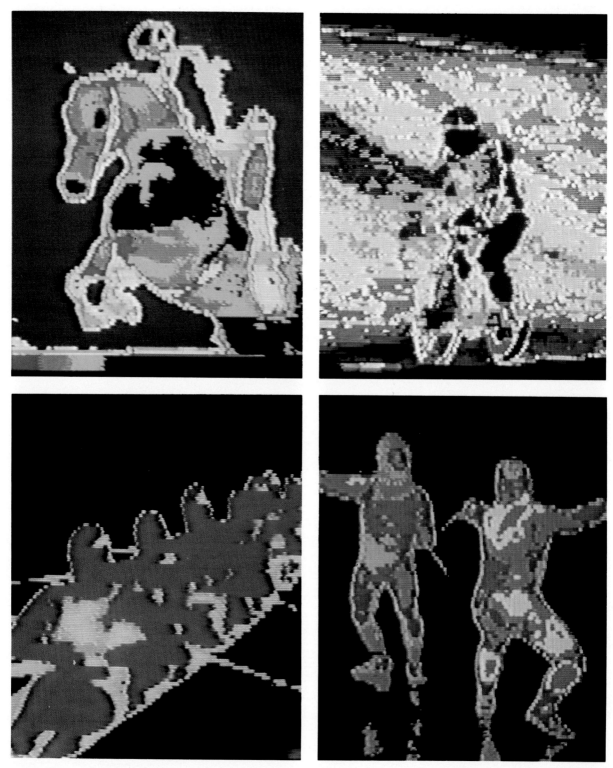

Using a chemically cooled lens and advanced infrared imaging systems, Douglas Nelson combines art and science in these Thermographic images, revealing the body's exertions and the extension and contraction of muscles in action.

The images can be modeled on a computer to analyze movements and forces and improve performance. (Thermographic images courtesy of Douglas B. Nelson, © 1983 Douglas B. Nelson.)

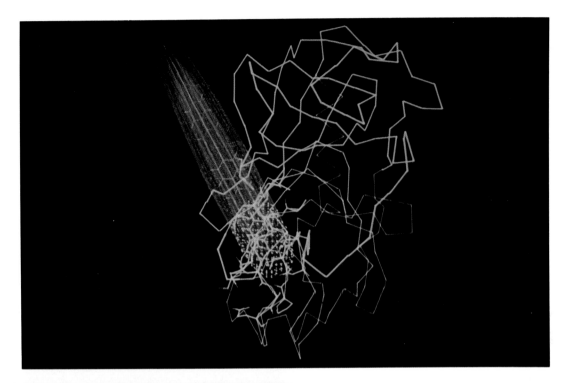

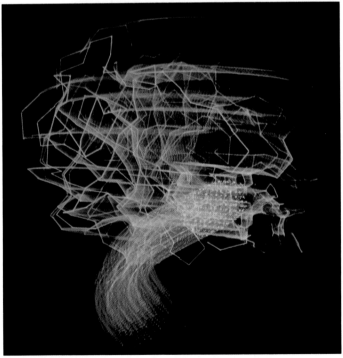

The luminescent trail was produced by exposing the film to a series of successive screen images to show the animation capability of a computer graphics system using a single still photograph. In one snapshot **(top)**, the protein macro-molecule holds still and the surface model of the inhibitor moves forward for "docking." In another snapshot **(bottom)**, the large protein molecule is rotating at the same time that the inhibitor is "docking." (Courtesy of Evans & Sutherland and Merck Sharp & Dohme Research Laboratories, and Merck and Co., Inc., Rahway, New Jersey, USA.)

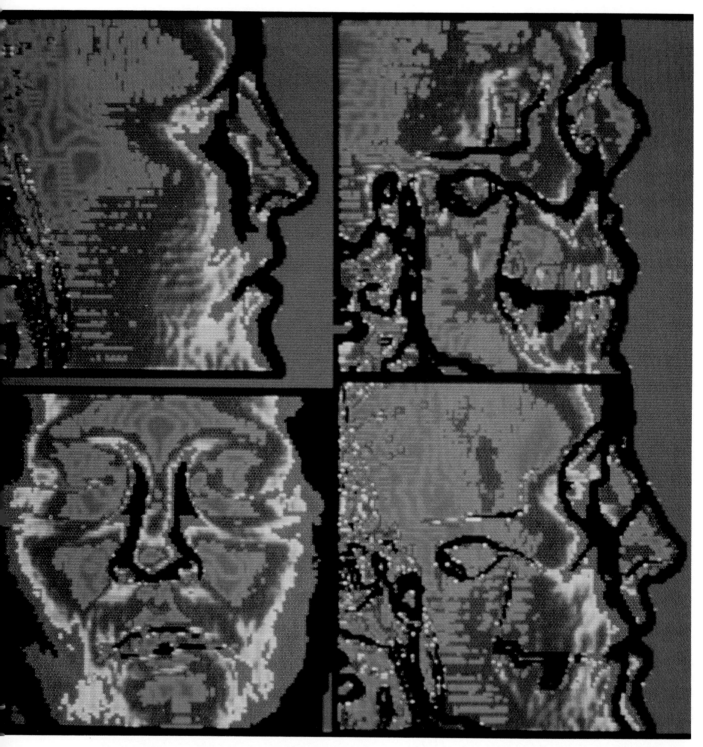

Flesh and bone both take on an eerie glow from the purple and gold colors in these CT scan reconstructions. **Lower left:** frontal view of the face. **Upper left:** right lateral view of the face. **Upper right:** surface of the skull of a living patient as "seen" by the CT scanner. **Lower right:** The computer has created an image in which the skull appears to be covered with transparent skin, so the bones of the skull are visible as well as the patient's nose, chin, and ear. (Courtesy of Mallinckrodt Institute, Washington University School of Medicine, St. Louis.)

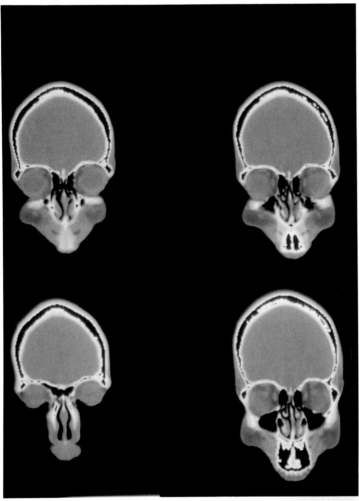

Computer tomography gives the radiologist extra-sensitive control over the exact portion of the body to investigate, and affords the chance to manipulate the x-ray results digitally to enhance discrimination of anatomical structures. Here, four views of the skull are presented. (Courtesy of Gould DeAnza.)

Pixel intensity values in the original computerized tomography (CT) scan of the lower abdomen (top right) are transformed into a relief image (bottom left), demonstrating the capability of image processing systems to construct a three-dimensional model from sufficient two-dimensional input data. (Courtesy of Comtal/3M, Altadena, California.)

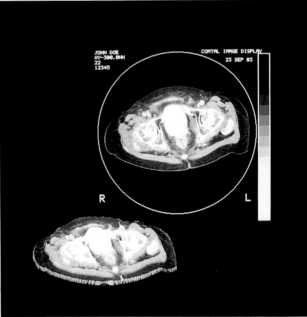

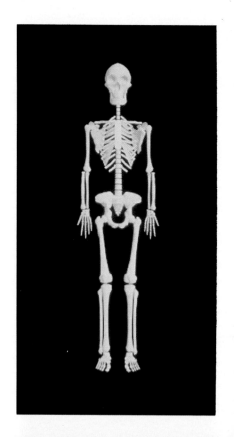

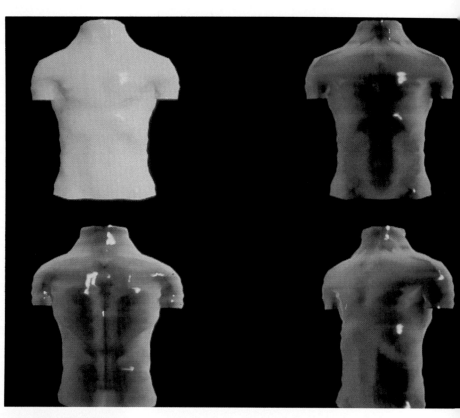

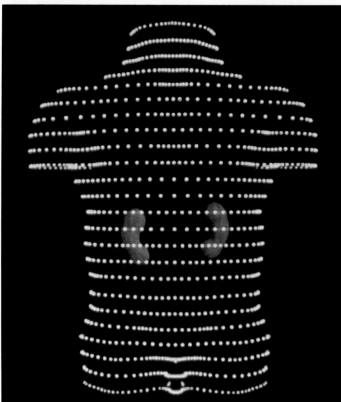

Solid and transparent views of the human anatomy are the products of computer animation. The illustrations were produced for *The Body Machine*, a television documentary on the day-to-day workings of a healthy human body. (Courtesy of Cranston-Csuri Productions, Inc.)

Above: Skeleton, with torso rendered as opaque and transparent (top) and in a vector pattern with kidneys positioned (bottom). Animators: Don Stredney and, for vector pattern, Jose Garabis.

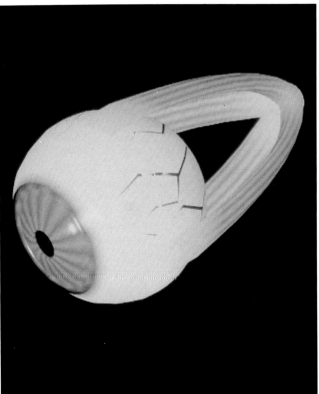

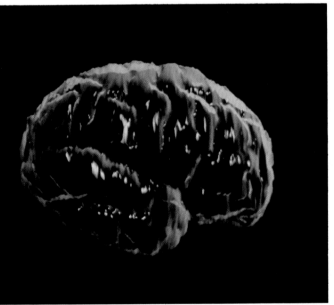

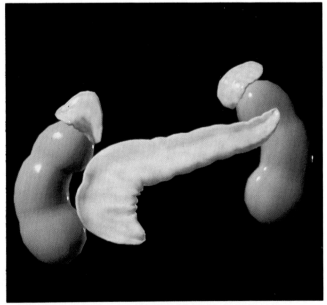

Clockwise from top left: Blood cells absorbing carbon dioxide, human eye, kidneys with adrenal glands and pancreas, and the human brain (transparent). Animators: Blood cells, Susan Van Baerle; eye and brain, Don Stredney; kidneys, Jose Garabis.

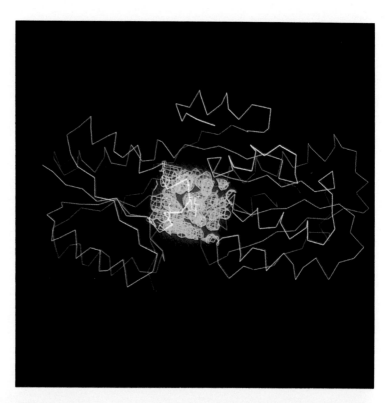

Biochemists study these orange and yellow webworks which describe portions of the molecular structure of a sugar-binding protein. In these views the computer has eliminated the clutter of the many atoms comprising the molecule by constructing the model according to the locations and arrangements of alphacarbon atoms only. The blue electron density maps indicate the sugar-binding region of the protein. (Courtesy of Evans & Sutherland and Rice University.)

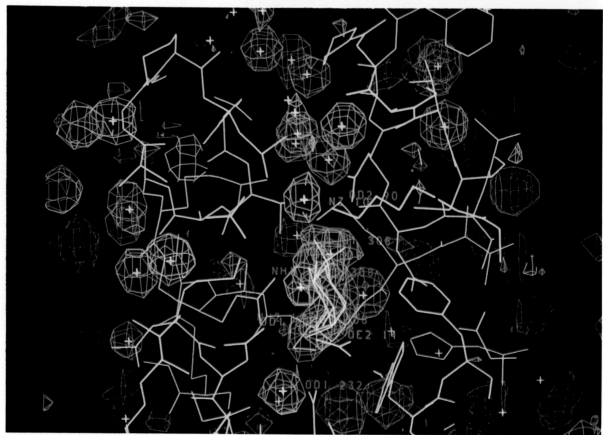

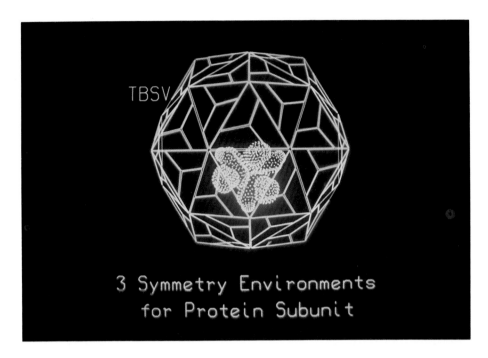

The vaulted framework **(above)** is a geometric representation of the locations of 180 protein subunits in the outer envelope of TBSV (tomato bushy stunt virus). One triangle has been replaced with a more detailed model, with dots indicating the surface of three subunits, each having two domains. This image from the movie *Virus Wars* shows the capability of GRAMPS software to model the molecular surface.

Below: A more detailed look at the surface of one domain reveals a multitude of lumps, due to the presence of individual atoms in the molecule. Acidic portions, having a negative charge, are shown in blue. The remainder are orange. White indicates overlay of blue and orange. (Courtesy of Evans & Sutherland and the Research Institute of Scripps Clinic.)

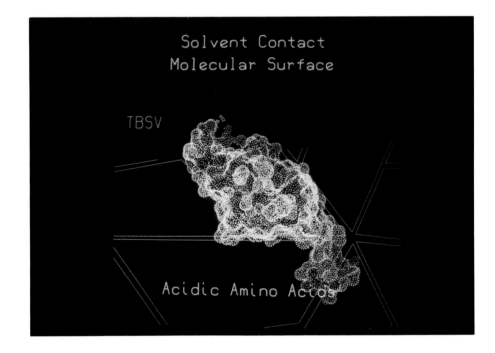

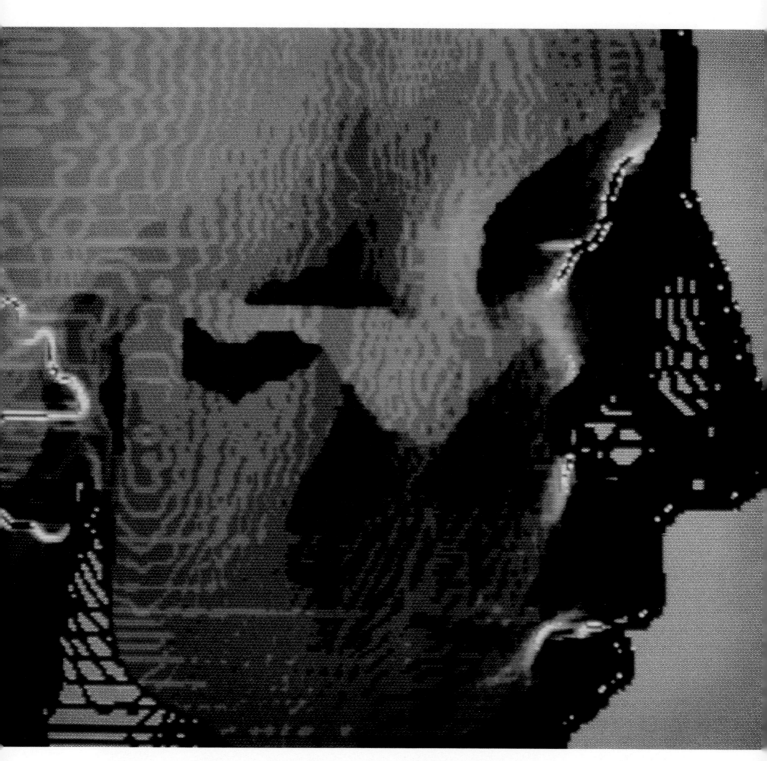

The face of an accident victim is studied with high-resolution CT scans to reveal the bony structure of the skull. (Courtesy of Mallinckrodt Institute, Washington University School of Medicine, St. Louis.)

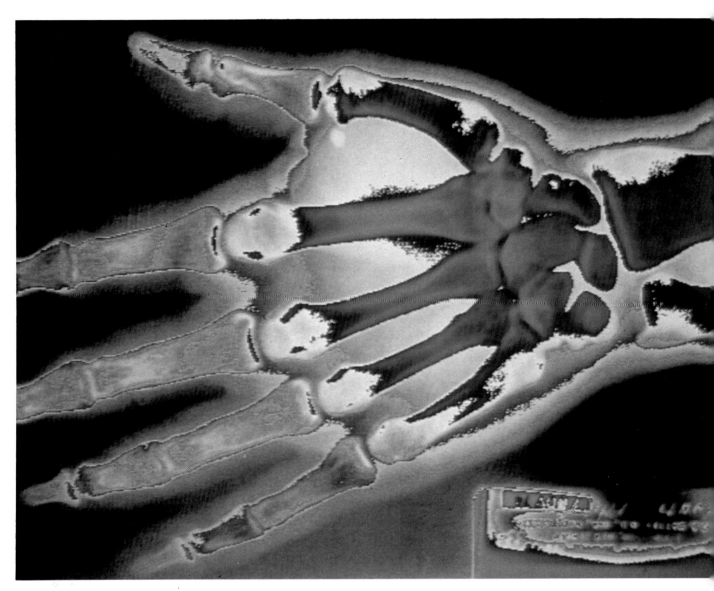

An x-ray film was digitized from black-and-white video camera input and subsequently pseudo-colored according to varying bone density to create this artistic piece titled *X-Hand*. Here, serious image-processing technology is used for sheer aesthetics. (Courtesy of Digital Graphic Systems, Inc.)

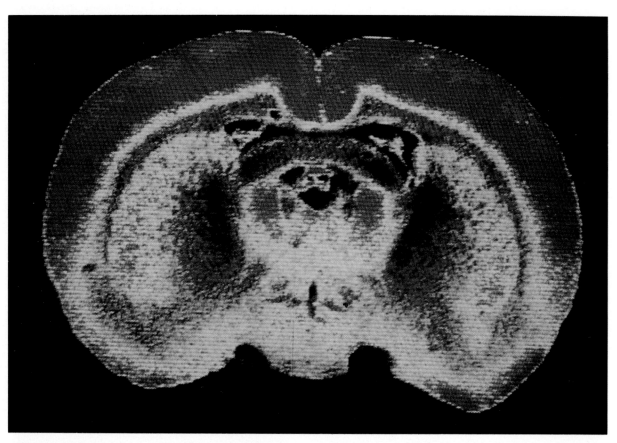

Above: The balance of chemicals within the brain is a significant factor in certain diseases. In this study the transport of three amino acids across the blood-brain barrier of individual brain structures was measured using laboratory rats. The method involved a brief infusion of labeled amino acid in tracer quantity, followed by quantitative autoradiography, yielding this image. Colors indicate tracer concentration within regions of the brain. (Courtesy of Optronics International, Inc.)

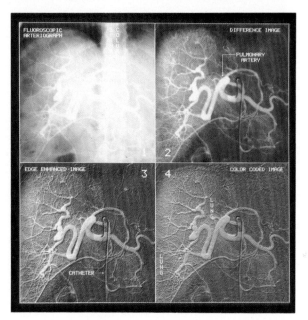

Left: Follow the steps that the radiologist took to emphasize the capillaries of the lung. To begin, an ordinary x-ray of the lung was made (not shown). Then, contrast material was injected through a catheter into the pulmonary artery and another x-ray was made (upper left). These two films were digitized and a "difference image" was obtained by subtracting one digital image from the other. Notice that the spinal column and all other common anatomical features are removed, leaving only the vascular system of the lung (upper right). The "difference image" was then edge-enhanced (lower left). A false color (pseudo-color) display was produced by using the "difference image" in red, the edge-enhanced image in green, and their average image in blue to photograph a composite (lower right). (Courtesy of Optronics International, Inc.)

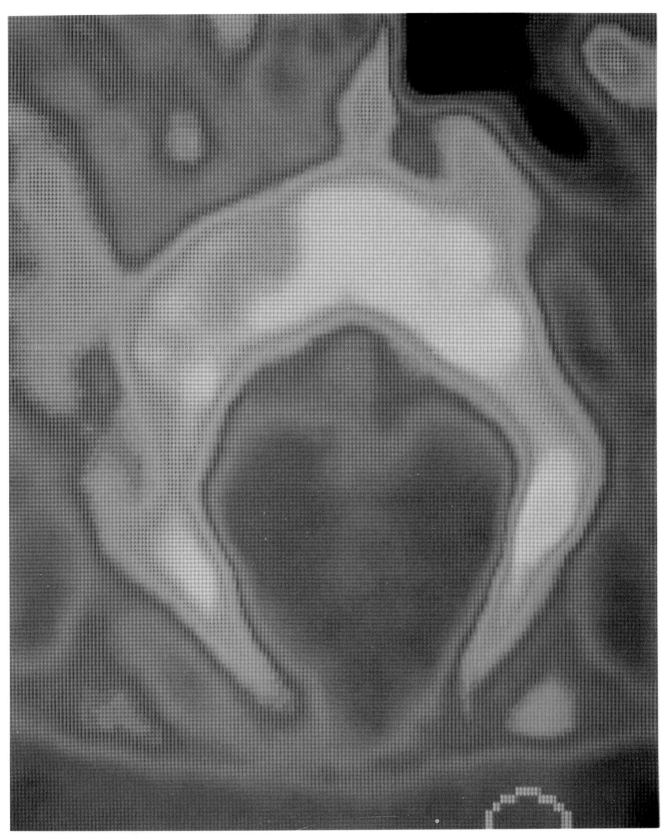

Computerized axial tomography of spina bifida and lipoma (fatty tumor) of the back extending into the spinal canal of a young child. The fatty tumor is red on the display. (Courtesy of the Department of Radiology, St. Luke's Episcopal and Texas Children's Hospitals and the Texas Heart Institute, Houston.)

The distance between the two eyes in a human face causes each eye to see a slightly different view of a real object, and the result is depth perception. Here, the computer has been programmed to generate two images having that same slight difference, creating this "stereo pair." An experienced biochemical researcher knows how to stare at a stereo image until the brain perceives it as a three-dimensional object. This stereo pair shows a dot-simulated molecular surface and the stick model of two sugars

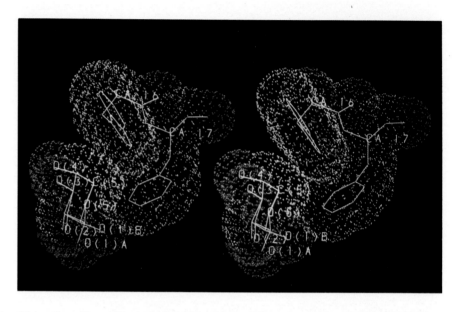

and side chains. The atoms in this molecule are identified with color as follows: carbon is green, nitrogen blue, and oxygen red. (Courtesy of Dr. F. A. Quiocho, Rice University.)

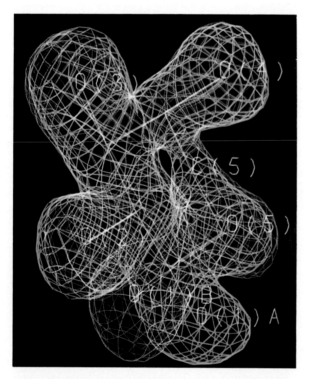

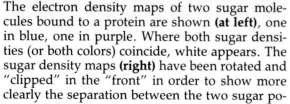

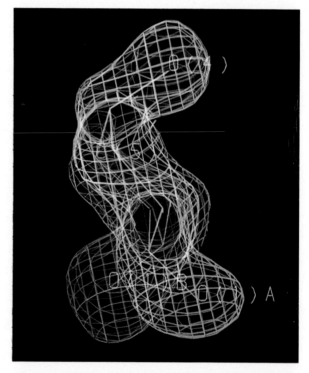

The electron density maps of two sugar molecules bound to a protein are shown **(at left)**, one in blue, one in purple. Where both sugar densities (or both colors) coincide, white appears. The sugar density maps **(right)** have been rotated and "clipped" in the "front" in order to show more clearly the separation between the two sugar positions and the accurate fit of the refined sugar model to corresponding density. All portions of the molecules closer to the "front" than a defined clipping plane were removed, leaving two "holes" where it is possible to look into the model. (Courtesy of Dr. F.A. Quiocho, Rice University.)

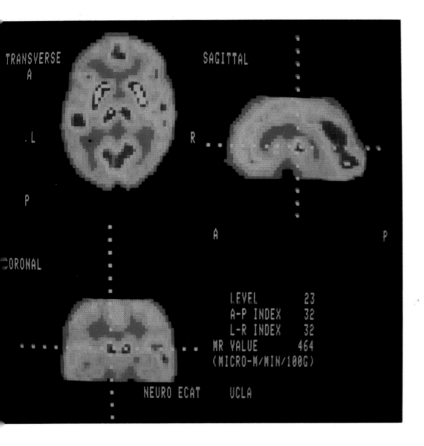

TRANSVERSE
A

.L   R

P

CORONAL   A   P

LEVEL   23
A-P INDEX   32
L-R INDEX   32
MR VALUE   464
(MICRO-M/MIN/100G)

NEURO ECAT   UCLA

SAGITTAL

Positron emission tomography (PET) is a relatively new addition to nuclear medicine. It is an even more powerful diagnostic tool when coupled with color graphics. These images show glucose uptake for points throughout the brain, distilling all data to a pseudo-colored slice across the brain. White-red-yellow shows high glucose uptake and thus high metabolic activity. Green-blue-purple shows lower values. The brain imagery divided into "transverse," "sagittal," and "coronal" planes demonstrates an additional function of the software. These three brain planes are kept in different storage areas of the image processor, and are exhibited in three different quadrants of the screen. Movement of the computer cursor over the screen allows a reading of brain glucose uptake at any plane throughout the brain. (Courtesy of Tony Ricci, Laboratory of Nuclear Medicine, UCLA, and Gould DeAnza.)

This color-coded display of phase and amplitude of cardiac chambers was obtained by the imaging of red blood cells tagged with a radio-isotope tracer. The accompanying graph was generated using Fourier analyses. (Courtesy of the Department of Radiology, Hermann Hospital, Houston.)

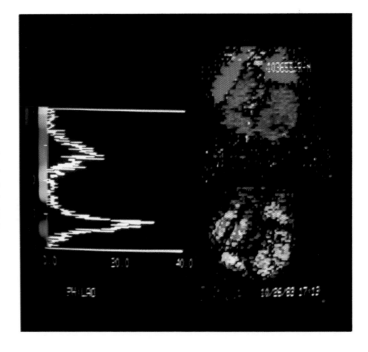

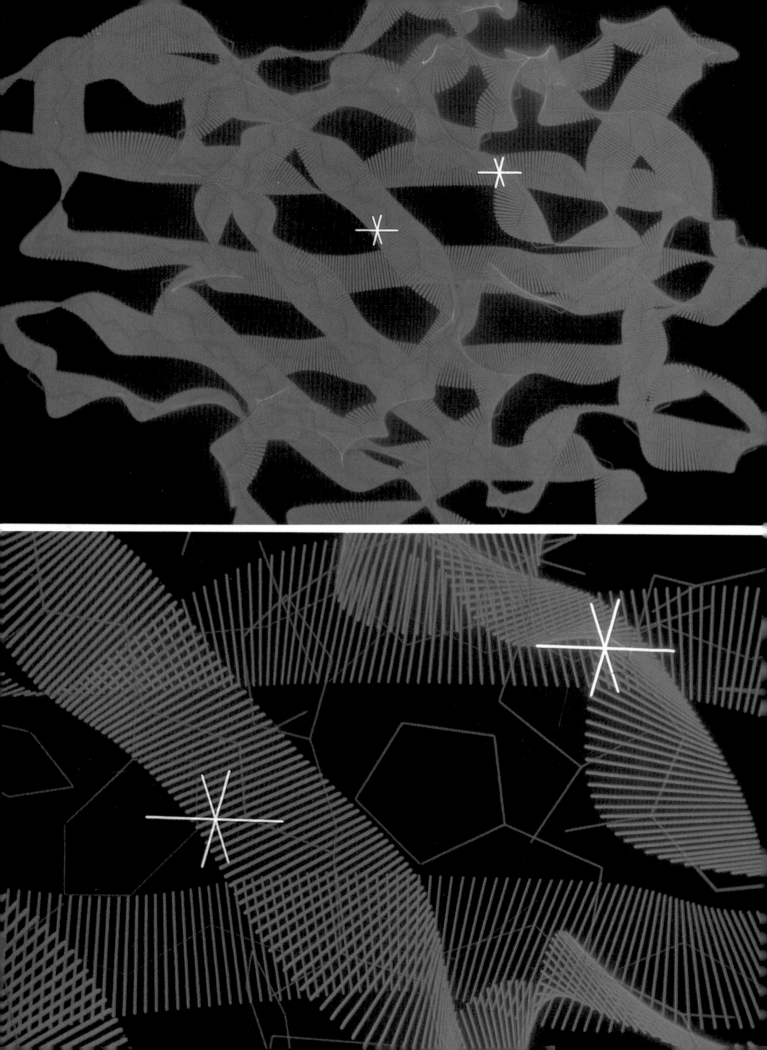

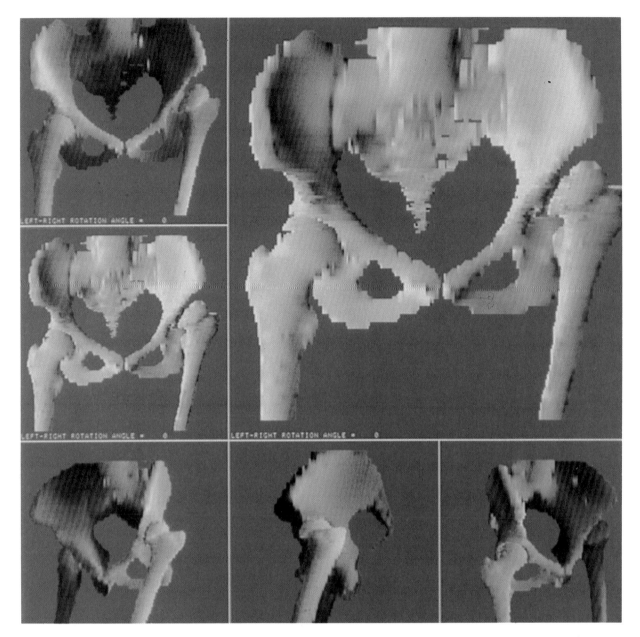

Congenital displacement of the hip, reconstructed from the patient's computerized tomography scan data. (Courtesy of Contour Medical Systems.)

Opposite: A maze of blue ribbons and red thread is in reality a molecule of the enzyme copper-zinc superoxide dismutase. (Enzymes are proteins that serve as catalysts for chemical reactions within the body.) **Top:** An overall view in which two white symbols represent the locations of the copper and the zinc atoms. **Bottom:** A close-up view of an area of interest around the copper and zinc locations. (Courtesy of Evans & Sutherland and the University of North Carolina.)

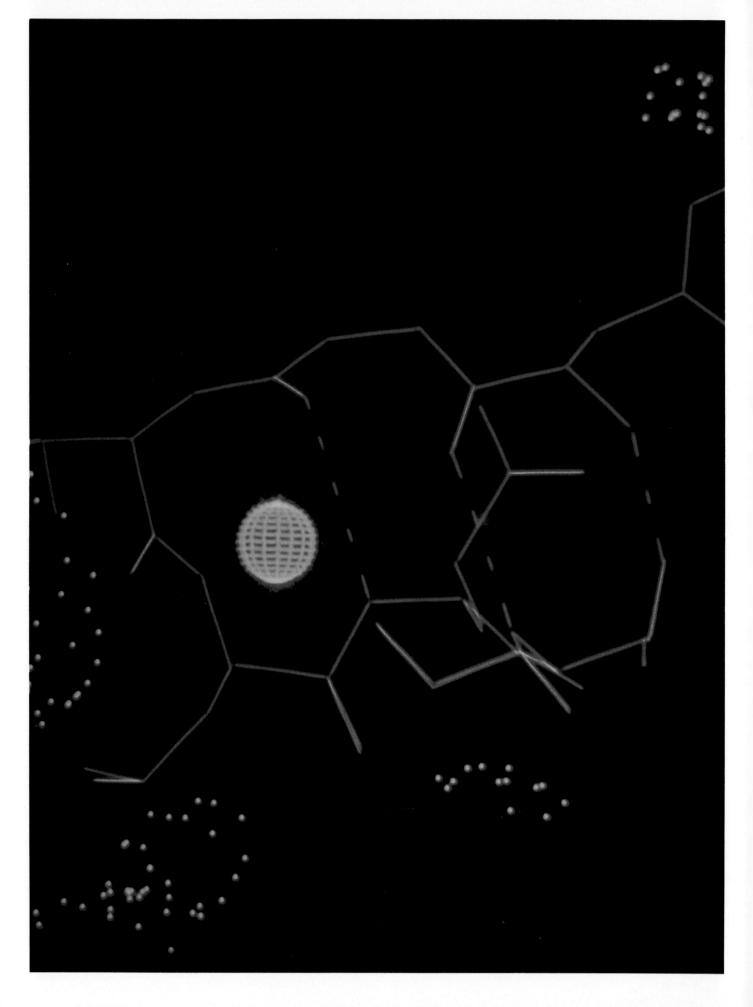

A DNA molecule. Red represents oxygen; blue, nitrogen; green, carbon; yellow, phosphorus; and white, hydrogen. (Courtesy of the Computer Graphics Laboratory, University of California, San Francisco. © Regents of the University of California.)

Opposite: The way the sequence of amino acids determines the three-dimensional shape of a protein molecule is the subject of computer-aided research. The solid lines correspond to covalent chemical bonds and the broken lines to hydrogen bonds. The sphere marks the position of a buried water molecule. The stippled blue surface traces the solvent-accessible surface of the protein. (Courtesy of Evans & Sutherland and the Hershey Medical Center.)

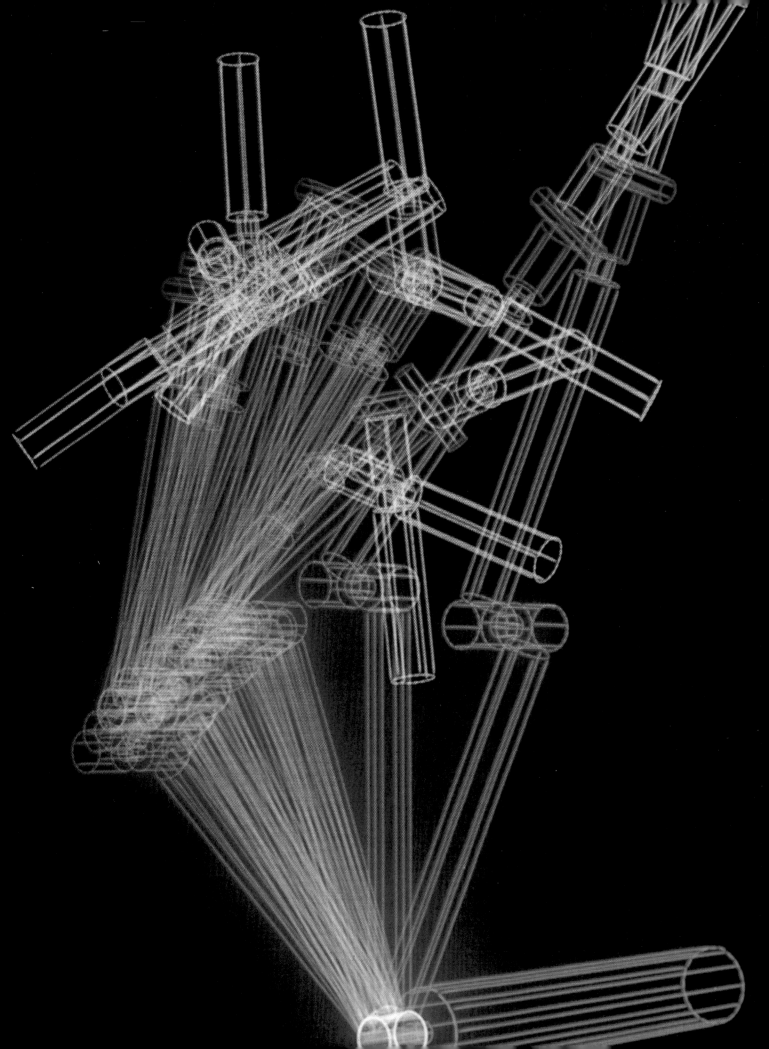

3. INVENTION

Scot Carpenter

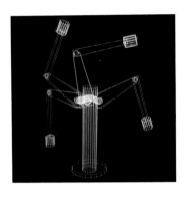

Man the inventor. Our history is recorded in the relics of inventions, from shards of pottery and the fragments of stone tools to the crumbling foundations of ancient buildings. Myths surround our early inventions: the Seven Wonders, the Trojan horse, the failure of Babel, the tragedy of Icarus. Invention is the realization of our dreams; it gives them substance and purpose.

Whether the first invention was a weapon, a tool, a shelter, or clothing does not matter: a process began that changed our relationship with the earth. We became manipulators of our world, architects, engineers, artisans, builders. And as our inventions grew more advanced and complex, our methods evolved. Design became more important and the graphic representation of our inventions, through plans and models, became a necessary part of the process.

The graphic language of invention, as expressed in architectural plans, working drawings, the sketches of daVinci, changed slowly from Roman times. Methods evolved, paper was developed, the graphite pencil replaced the scriber. But even so, a draftsman from the early nineteenth century would soon have felt at home in a mid-twentieth century design office. Twenty years ago his skills and concepts would have been current. That was before the digital electronic computer had its impact on the design process.

Opposite: This robotic simulation conveys a sense of magical motion in soft colors. A dynamic analysis is performed on a computer model consisting of six parts and five joints. The first two joints from the left are specified as torsion springs, the last three are designated as frictionless bearings. Gravity is calculated to be acting along the vertical axis of the pedestal. This multi-frame photograph shows the range of dynamic action when the system is released. (Courtesy of Evans & Sutherland and Mechanical Dynamics, Inc.)

"Cosine curve" modeled in three-dimensions using the SOLIDVIEW™ system. (Courtesy of Lexidata.)

Eniac, the first digital computer, began operating in 1946. Early applications in computer-aided design (CAD) were primarily computational, with no graphic output. Numerical control (NC), the automated control of machine tools, was developed at MIT in the early 1950s. By the mid-1960s there were several CAD systems in use at large companies such as General Motors and Boeing, but there were no standard graphics programs. Each system was a specialized design and required a large "mainframe" computer to support it.

These early systems were used for sophisticated design and analysis as well as for generating graphic images and drawings. Smaller companies needed systems to automate their drafting departments but could not afford the mainframe CAD systems. By the early 1970s advances in computer technology made minicomputer-based CAD systems possible. Vendors began offering "turnkey" systems at a fraction of the price of older systems. Turnkey vendors offered a complete CAD system from one source. This allowed companies without large data processing departments to install a system and be assured of support.

Turnkey systems gave CAD a new meaning—computer-aided drafting. The minicomputer CAD systems could not perform the sophisticated design and analysis of a mainframe system, but they could speed up the design and drafting process and increase the productivity of drafting departments. These productivity gains are typically in the area of three to one but can be more than ten to one for certain operations.

Soon companies using computer-aided drafting systems began to realize the wealth of information contained in a set of architectural plans or an engineering drawing. Computer-aided design and drafting became the new phrase and more sophisticated graphics and analysis capabilities were offered. With the current move to "super-minicomputers," we are seeing the design and analysis capabilities once limited to General Motors and Boeing becoming available to the more than 3,000 owners of turnkey CAD systems.

The newest development in CAD is the desktop system. Since its inception in 1972, the microprocessor chip has increased incredibly in power. Today's newest 16- and 32-bit microprocessors are equal in computational speed to the large minicomputers of a few years ago. This has made possible desktop computers with graphics capabilities that can run full-featured CAD software. Some manufacturing industries have already moved to essentially "paperless" design, with the computer-produced design being used to generate the numerical control program which automatically produces the part. The desktop system will soon become as common on an engineer's desk as a calculator is today.

Merging computer-aided design and computer-aided manufacturing into computer-integrated manufacturing (CIM) promises to be the next step in our move to a post-industrial information society. The proliferation of microprocessor-based workstations and the process of networking these computers into an integrated system will take years, but the effects will cause fundamental changes in our society and the way we work. Many experts are predicting that automating the manufacturing process will pull the United States out of its productivity slump. The unanswered question is what effect this automation will have on the American worker.

The techniques used in CAD are applications of more general computer graphics methods. The first systems used vector representations for the objects being drawn. This method of drawing lines on a graphics display is still used and has many advantages. It is analogous to manual drawing techniques and is easy to learn. It lends itself to vector manipulation methods and to pen-plotted output. It is well suited for drafting and can be used for both two- and three-dimensional images.

Most CAD images are vector representations. These are typically "wire frames," with the edges of the object shown by lines. There are some serious problems with three-dimensional wire-frame representations. Since only the edges are shown, cylindrical features must have some additional processing to define their boundaries. Wire frames are inherently transparent; this leads to ambiguities in viewing which make it difficult to discern near from far surfaces. To overcome this problem, an entire area of computer graphics has struggled with the "hidden line" problem in attempts to efficiently determine which lines we should not be able to see. In addition to the viewing ambiguities, wire frames have structural ambiguities; they tell us nothing about the surfaces or volumes of the objects we are modeling.

Surface and solid modeling techniques remove the viewing ambiguity problem. Surface modeling techniques define the object by its surfaces, rather than its edges. On a vector display the surface can be shown by a mesh or network of lines, on a raster display the surface can appear as a shaded area.

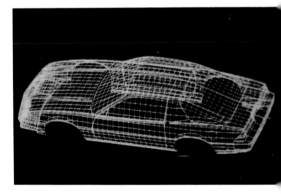

A mesh of polygons specifies the curved surfaces of an automobile body. (Courtesy of Spectragraphics.)

A simulated torus rendered in copper and obsidian. This image is a superior example of realistic surfacing and perspective. (Courtesy of David Salesin, Department of Computer Science, Brown University.)

By using perspective, shadow-casting, and shading techniques, images of near-photographic quality can be generated. Solid modeling techniques go even further toward a realistic model of the object. The object is defined by volumes, hence the term solid modeling. The model can be built up by defining simple solid shapes such as cubes, cylinders, spheres, etc., and then combining these simple shapes to make more complex objects. This is an involved process, and CAD vendors are developing methods of improving the solid-model generation process.

Once a solid model has been defined, incredible applications are possible. Shaded, realistic images can be generated. Section views can be made from any angle. Analysis can be done for mass properties, moments of inertia, etc. Numerical control programs can develop the operations necessary to machine a part. Solid modeling holds tremendous promise for the future of computer graphics and design.

To take full advantage of the capabilities of CAD systems, the information *about* the object being displayed must be considered. Architectural plans and engineering drawings contain tremendous amounts of information. This non-graphic data may appear on the drawing as notes, dimensions, labels, etc., or it may not be on the drawing at all, but associated with it in a database. Application programs that access this data can do analyses, generate bills of material, be used for inventory control or production scheduling. As information systems become more sophisticated, CAD will be integrated into a company's total management information system.

Applications for CAD are growing constantly. In one of its earliest homes, the manufacturing industry, the close tolerances and need for greater productivity in making increasingly complex shapes led to the development of numerical control. It thus has been a natural extension to use computer-aided techniques to create the initial design. New developments in manufacturing include automating parts-handling and assembly with industrial robots. The graphic simulation of robot movement and using simulations to program robots is a new area for computer-aided design.

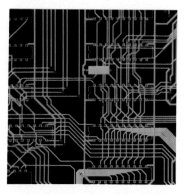

Computers and color graphics facilitate design and production of complex printed circuit boards. (Courtesy of Spectragraphics.)

An interesting quirk of high technology electronics is that the large-scale integrated circuits used in CAD systems are themselves designed with CAD. Indeed, it is now impossible to produce these chips without using computers. As very large-scale integrated (VLSI) circuits become extremely complex, with more and more layers of very dense micro-circuits stacked together, computer-aided design methods are a necessity. Some of the newest microprocessors have several hundred thousand components on a single fingernail-sized chip. Manufacturing such chips requires a highly automated, carefully controlled environment. Some of the newest graphics workstations use specialized chips to perform the graphic manipulations normally done by programs. Such "graphics engines" are making the dynamic display of realistic images more common. We will see specialized chips implemented to handle more and more of the operations currently done by software programs. This will result in faster, more economical CAD systems and more complex designs.

The manufacture of these complex designs requires the precision of computer-controlled processes. Circuit paths are separated by a few thousandths of an inch and must be etched into the silicon of the chip under extremely clean, critically controlled conditions. As the design and production of these chips becomes more sophisticated, we will reach a point where our own ideas and concepts become so advanced that we will be unable to realize or implement them without computers. And though we have not yet reached the point of computers designing and building themselves, the idea is no fantasy.

Many of the most beautiful examples of computer graphics come from the field of architecture. With the emergence of low-cost CAD systems, architecture has become a high-growth area for computer applications. Firms ranging from two partners to the giants of the architectural, engineering and construction industries such as Bechtel and Brown & Root have embraced CAD. The systems used vary from the simplest—some based on Apple computers—to million-dollar systems networked across the continent. Architects were quick to see the promise of surface and solid modeling and some firms now videotape the computer images produced on their systems. Such presentations can show realistic images of exteriors, interiors, or an imaginary flight through the proposed site of the new project.

CAD in architecture is more than presentation graphics. While the design of a building wins contracts and awards, the practical elements of architecture make a building serve its purpose. The computer provides new graphic and analytical tools for facility planning, environmental analysis, heat load calculations, and construction cost estimating. Archi-

A three-dimensional office interior photographed from the screen of a color graphics workstation. (Courtesy of Intergraph.)

tects can use the same three-dimensional shaded surface programs that show the exterior of buildings to create realistic images of office interiors, down to papers on the desk and plants in the corner. They can mix and match colors and light sources, and select from standard furniture and fixtures.

Open design concepts give facility planners tremendous flexibility. With CAD, planners no longer have to move cardboard cutouts around blueprints; CAD allows them to rearrange entire floors graphically. They can give check-prints of various arrangements to their clients or, with a three-dimensional system, present a simulated walk through the building.

The applications of CAD are limited only by the architect's imagination and creativity. Firms have used medical computerized tomography scanners to produce computer models from miniature sculptor's models so that accurate construction drawings could be made. One firm used their system to demonstrate to city officials that their new building would not cast shadows on the beach across the street. CAD gives architects the freedom to explore new and more daring designs and the means to realize them.

Computer graphics in design and production is bringing basic changes in the way we work. The skills of drawing and lettering are being replaced by workstation operation and keyboard typing. Greater attention must be paid to the types of information we are dealing with, because design and production information is being stored in databases for data processing purposes. New workstations will be smaller, perhaps lap-sized, with full-color flat displays. As CAD systems become more powerful, engineers and architects will work directly with them. These changes will mean job displacement: Whole categories of work dealing with the production and handling of engineering and architectural drawings will be replaced by information processing jobs. Workers, including professionals, will have to learn new skills every few years.

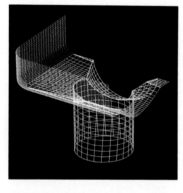

This three-dimensional surface model of a mechanical design shows meshing, trimming, filleting, and complex intersections. (Courtesy of Intergraph.)

We are inventors. Our greatest inventions transcend utility to merge art and technology. The process of invention has not changed—the key element is still the creative drive in a human being. Computers have expanded the tools we have available; they allow us to see our dreams in electronic images, and this is a creative freedom we have never known before. There will be inventions more fantastic than Leonardo's, waiting only for science to achieve what we have already conceived.

The premier U.S. Air Force fighter, the F-15, is modeled here in an image taken from a detailed, animated, interactive flight simulator. As the plane maneuvers in response to the pilot trainee's actions, the appearance of the ground below changes. This state-of-the-art flight simulator will be used to evaluate the pilot's capability in limited-field-of-view situations, and to demonstrate the effects of air-to-air missiles and other weapons, for tactical mission training. (Courtesy of Evans & Sutherland.)

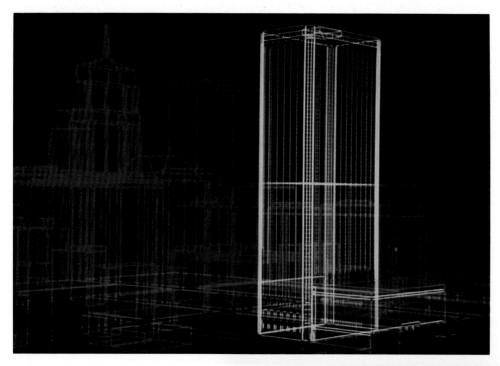

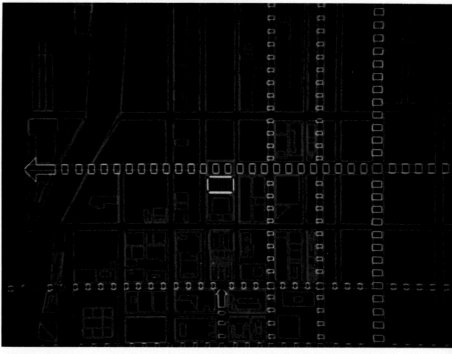

Skyline planning—architects can now critique the profile of a proposed building **(top)** against an existing urban skyline. This new twist to the traditional task of site planning is a welcome tool in today's complicated, congested metropolises, and it is only made possible through computer graphics. The perspective view is presented as a wire-frame image, thus the front, back, top, and bottom of the building are all visible. The corresponding plan view **(bottom)** is generated from the same computer database. A traffic analysis of the effect of the project on its urban environment has been added (white). (Courtesy of Evans & Sutherland and Skidmore, Owings and Merrill, Chicago.)

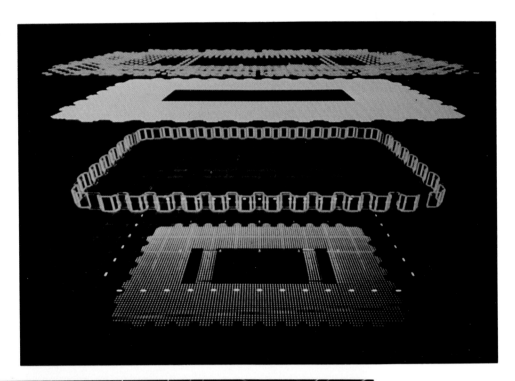

Color is used to delineate design components in these images from a three-dimensional construction planning system. The **top** image is an exploded view of the layers of data used to describe a single floor in a typical office building. The term "layer" helps the architect mentally construct the database codes that segregate various structural and mechanical systems, and it describes a common way of showing the separate systems. Inside the actual building the items on various layers may be side by side. The **bottom** image is an interior perspective of a typical office floor, showing systems in their respective locations—yellow ductwork in the ceiling, green exterior walls, white floor grid, red lines indicating interior partitions. (Courtesy of Evans & Sutherland and Skidmore, Owings and Merrill, Chicago.)

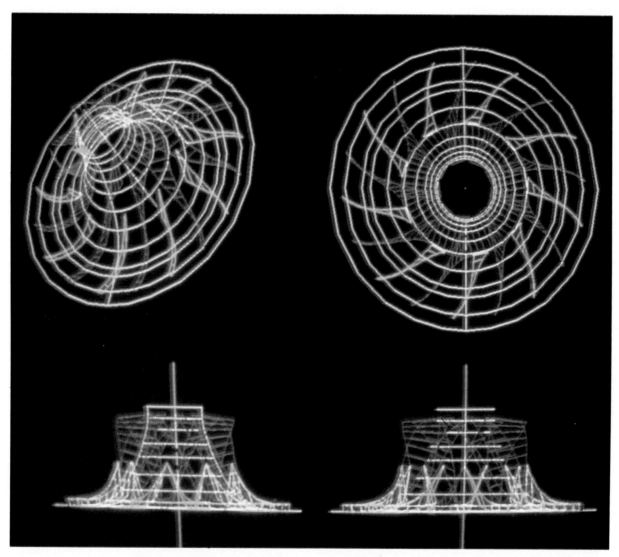

Colorful spinning pinwheels illustrate a serious three-dimensional design problem—the complex curved surfaces of the blades (alternately red and green) for the rotor of a centrifugal pump impeller. The design function, utilizing computer graphics, can be interfaced to the numerical calculations that check the efficiency and durability of the rotor. (Courtesy of Gerber Systems Technology, Inc.)

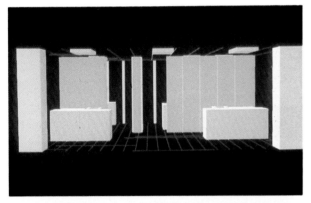
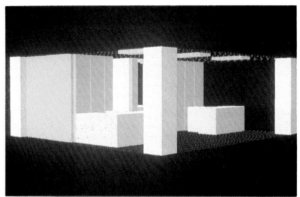
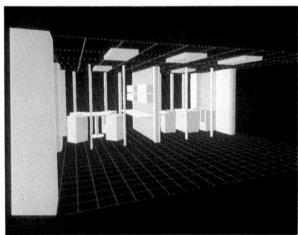
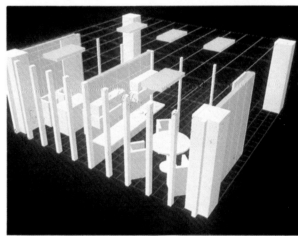

Lights, columns, partitions, and furniture—how much easier it is for the architect's client to visualize a design from these three-dimensional views than from paper cut-outs moved around on blueprints. Graphics systems optimize floor space and help create comfortable, efficient office arrangements that use common design elements like modular wall partitions situated in open areas. This image features just enough detail to make items recognizable without excessive geometry, which would slow down the generation of any desired view of the three-dimensional model. (Courtesy of Walker Associates, Inc. Created on a TRICAD Computer-Aided Design System.)

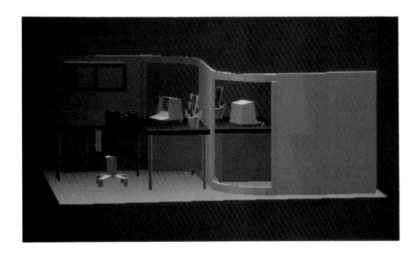

A realistic preview. Partitions and furniture arrangements can be visualized immediately and checked to determine if they satisfy a client's needs. (Courtesy of Sigma Design, Inc.)

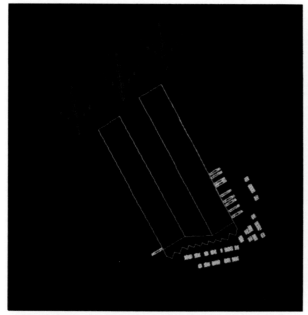

An air cargo terminal is modeled and tested before it is built to ensure unobstructed terminal access for cars, trucks, and airplanes. The computer model is accurately scaled, and each vehicle can be moved to various locations to imitate daily operations. The views generated from the model are wire-frame displays with hidden lines visible, the fastest display-generation method—well-suited to "quick looks" by professionals accustomed to working with graphics. An overhead view **(left)** gives the schematic site plan. An aerial perspective **(right)** imparts a feeling for the solid shapes. (Courtesy of The Office of Pierce Goodwin Alexander.)

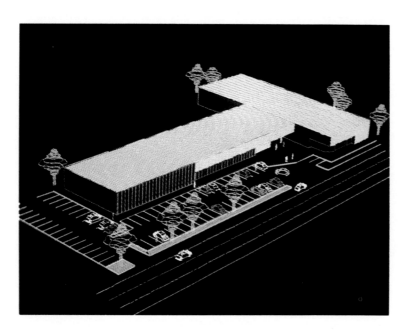

An architect sketches the exterior of a proposed building using as much or as little detail as is required. The flexibility of a three-dimensional modeling system in generating screen images from any selected point of view adds extra selling power. (Reprinted with permission from Computervision Corporation, Bedford, MA.)

A model building displayed in full perspective almost jumps into reality as the viewer is zoomed right up to the front door in this series of computer-generated images. Animator: Michael Collery. (Courtesy of Cranston-Csuri Productions, Inc.)

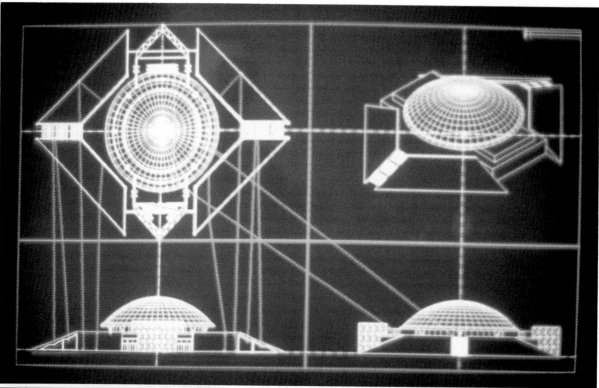

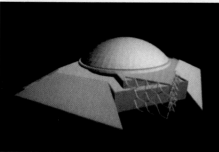

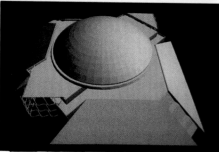

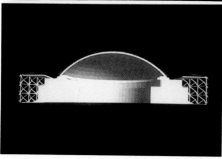

The "Spacehab" exhibit pavilion designed for the City of Tokyo is seen here in a series of screen images. In the large image **(above)**, the screen is split into four windows to demonstrate how the computer model was created. The user must define a minimum of two line-drawing profiles in different planes, then link the profiles together by means of common points. For this pavilion, three views were input: a plan view (upper left window), front elevation (lower left window), and back elevation (lower right window). The perspective (upper right window) was generated from the other views. Two types of links are displayed on this split-screen image. The dashed white lines define common horizontal and vertical axes for aligning the views. The turquoise lines define common points on the design to connect the multiple two-dimensional drawings into the single three-dimensional model shown in the three smaller images **(left)**. Here, two perspective views of the exterior and a cross section of the interior are shown. (Created by Bernardo Kraus under the direction of Elizabeth Bollinger. Courtesy of the Graduate Design Studio, College of Architecture, University of Houston.)

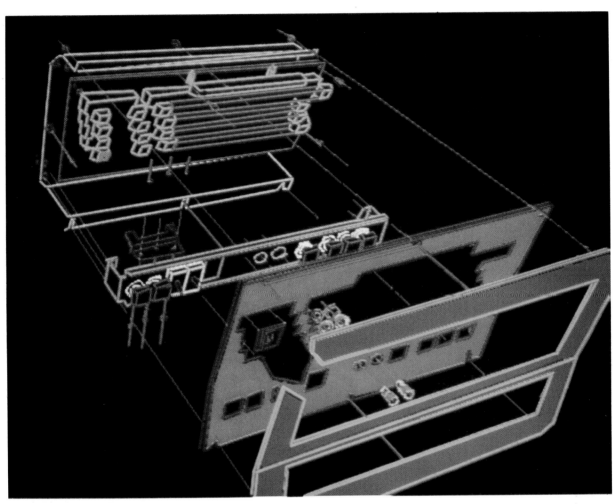

A colorful free-hand rendering of a keyboard design in an exploded view is effective in advertising, technical manuals, sales presentations, and other engineering illustrations. This image resembles an exploded view derived from an engineering model, giving a dynamic feel to a flat drawing. (Courtesy of Digital Graphic Systems, Inc.)

Exploded view of a mechanical assembly allows a clearer look at its components. (Courtesy of Spectragraphics.)

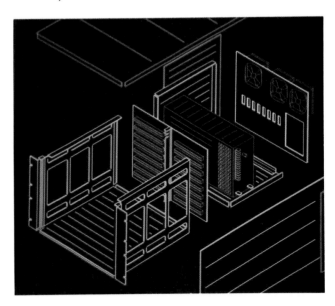

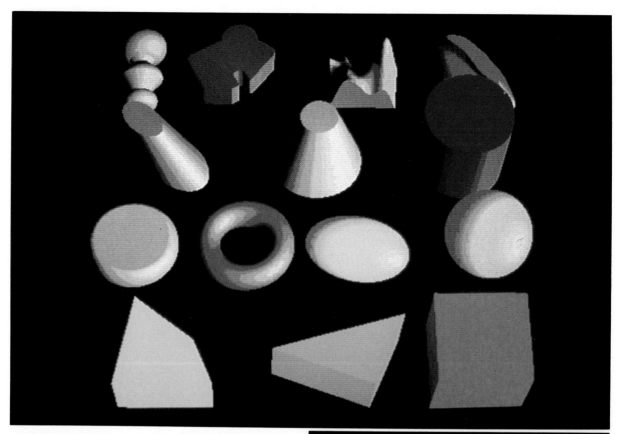

Building blocks. These glossy colored shapes are reminiscent of a set of toys, but they are actually the primitive shapes in an advanced solid modeling system **(top).** The concept is to begin with mathematically defined geometric solids: sphere, cube, truncated pyramid, and so forth. The computer program operates on the primitive solids in the same way a sculptor works with wood, clay or other materials: cutting, stretching, flattening, joining. One object can be used to make a hole in another—a smaller cylinder defined as a hole inside a larger cylinder yields a tube shape. The operations applied to the primitive shapes yield individual mechanical components **(middle),** which are joined together **(bottom)** to create a model of the assembled mechanism—a crankshaft.

The perfectly smooth contours of the sphere, ovoid, and ring are the result of the exact definition of the shapes (through equations), in contrast to methods that approximate curved surfaces using many flat elements. The slight jaggedness apparent in the image is due to the relatively low resolution of the screen, making the raster-scan lines large enough to be seen in the photograph. (Courtesy of Control Data Corporation.)

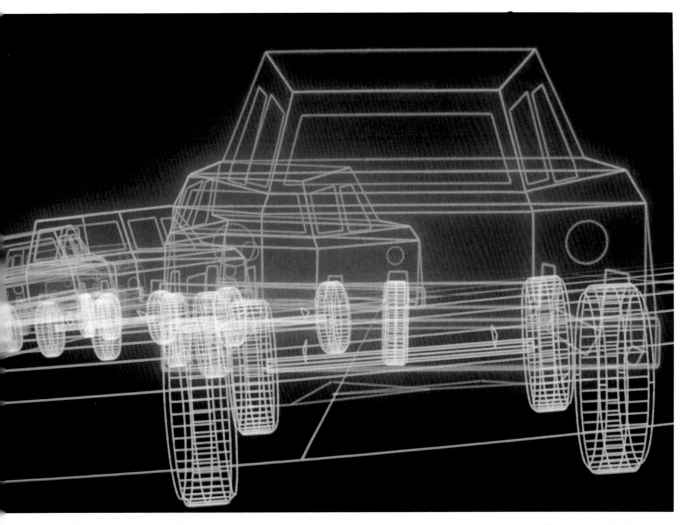

Bumpy roads, sharp turns, and quick lane changes test the mettle of this simulated Ford Bronco II. In the simulation, components such as steering, suspension, bushings, and tires are represented in detail. (Courtesy of Evans & Sutherland and Mechanical Dynamics, Inc.)

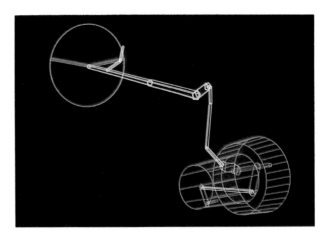

Kinematic analysis of a linkage mechanism is a classic exercise in mechanical engineering. The shift lever of a car or truck is mounted on the steering column (upper left), the gears are represented by wire-frame cylinders (lower right). This view of the three-dimensional model was photographed from a color, vector-drawing display. (Courtesy of Evans & Sutherland and Mechanical Dynamics, Inc.)

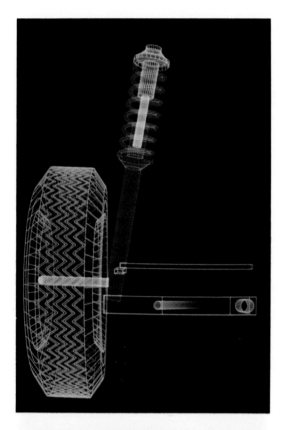

An automobile wheel and suspension are studied in this series of detailed line drawings. The designer has used colors to isolate and identify components within the three-dimensional model, and to give greater clarity to each view.

Left: The wheel is in a straight position, at rest. **Bottom right:** The wheel is in an extreme turn, again at rest. **Bottom left:** The wheel is in motion. The designer has programmed the computer graphics system with the equations needed to calculate circular motion. Many times per second, the graphics system calculates a new position for each short vector in the tire tread, according to the assumed speed, and immediately displays that vector in its new position. In the short time that the camera exposes the film to photograph the screen image, the lines in the tread are displayed in several locations, thus creating the blurred effect. (Courtesy of Evans & Sutherland.)

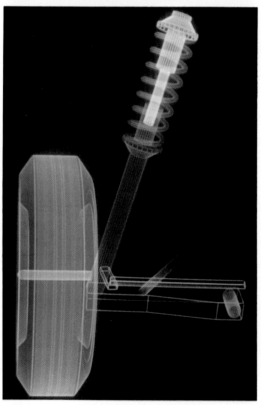

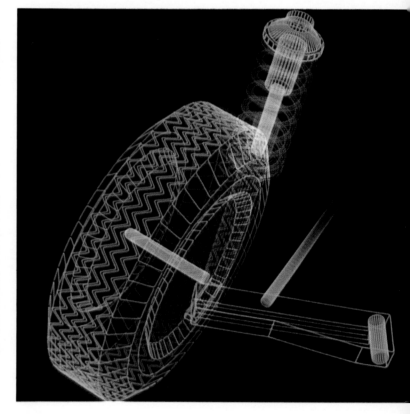

A mistake made behind the wheel may be fatal on the road, but it is a learning experience on the computer. These four scenes are from a graphics system that simulates typical situations in operating a motor vehicle. (It is a sophisticated cousin of the racetrack-driver video games.) In this application the amount of detail must be sufficient to give the driver a sense of reality, but limited to a manageable database so the computer can quickly respond to driver decisions with a new view of the road situation. This graphics system is used on a driving simulator to study driver behavior in critical situations and to optimize vehicle safety design. (Courtesy of Evans & Sutherland and Daimler-Benz.)

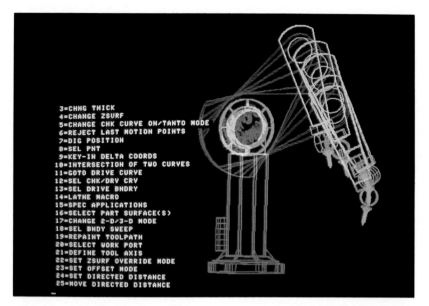

A numerically controlled (N/C) machine tool follows pre-programmed commands (rather than manual guiding by a machinist) in manufacturing products from wood, metal, and other materials. When the item is designed with a computer, semi-automatic generation of the N/C commands to control the manufacturing process is possible. The commands are edited and checked using an interactive system such as the one illustrated here. The colored image demonstrates the tool executing a proposed cutting path, a checking method that verifies the correctness of the commands without wasting expensive materials on trial runs. A pop-up menu listing commands available to the N/C programmer appears on the left. (Reprinted with permission from Computervision Corporation, Bedford, MA.)

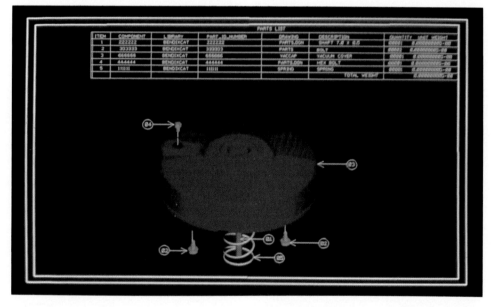

A realistic assembly drawing of a vacuum cover. The small numbers in circles, pointing to various parts of the device, are keyed to the parts list across the top. In the database, geometric information is associated with numeric and textual information. When a designer pulls the symbol for a part from the graphics library and places it on a drawing, the parts list information is compiled automatically. For construction, manufacturing, and documentation such as sales catalogs and maintenance manuals, this is a valuable by-product of computer-aided design. (Courtesy of Intergraph.)

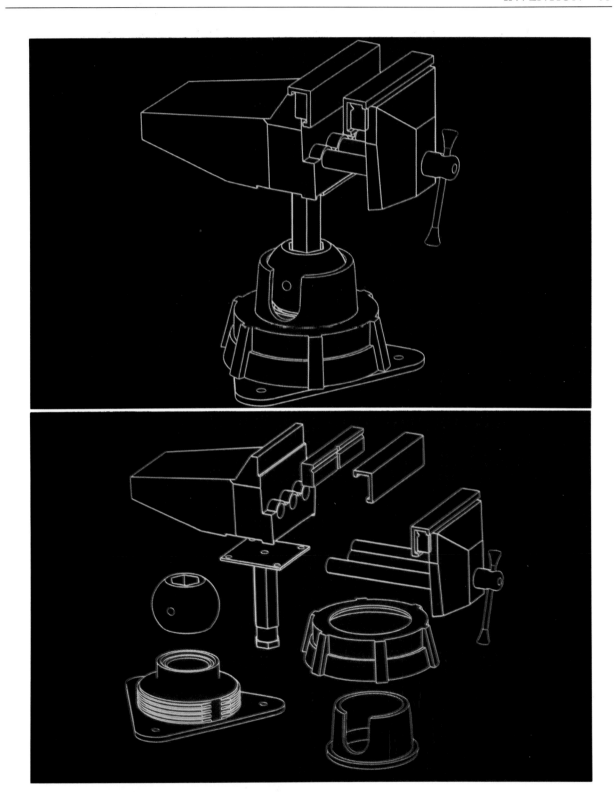

A vise **(top)** is displayed as a wire-frame image with hidden lines removed. In the exploded view **(bottom)** lines that were previously hidden are now visible, but within each component hidden lines are still removed. This display technique re-quires more data processing as each view is generated from the model in the database, but the result is a cleaner, clearer representation. (Courtesy of Evans & Sutherland and Shape Data, Ltd.)

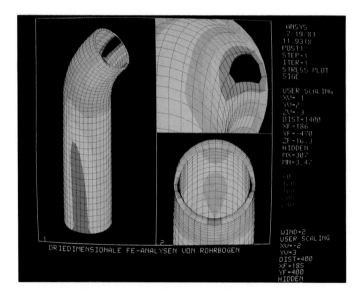

Color indicates the results of computations in this image, and therefore the color is output automatically by the computer system in accordance with a predetermined scale. The three windows show three different views at different distances from the object being studied, a pipe with a 45-degree elbow. The white grid divides the object into small units for finite element analysis. The display shows stress contours in color, with hidden surfaces removed for clarity. Computer graphics gives essential aid to mechanical engineers in interpreting the results of a complex analysis. (Courtesy of Swanson Analysis Systems, Inc. Generated by the finite element program ANSYS.®)

This is the way the building looks from across the street. But this street is located inside a graphics workstation at the architectural office, and the building's appearance is determined by solid-modeling software. (Reprinted with permission from Computervision Corporation, Bedford, MA.)

This Cheverolet Camaro is a synthetic electronic image, yet new computer techniques that simulate the lighting effects in a professional photographer's studio give it an extra touch of realism. Engineers evaluate the design of the automotive body even before a physical model of the car is built, and even the complex shapes of parts are visualized from numeric descriptions. In this system the geometric shape of any object is approximated by a three-dimensional mesh of polygons. Polygons can be grouped to form parts: For a car body there might be separate parts for the door, hood, roof, fender, etc. Each part is assigned a surface type, such as steel or glass, and each type of surface has associated color and reflectance properties. The entire data structure is stored in two tables, one for the mesh, another for surface and lighting parameters. This interactive system uses menus and screen selections to define parameters and options, to select a viewing orientation, or to mix a color. To generate a desired perspective, the computer eliminates those surfaces that would be hidden from view at that angle in reality. (Courtesy of General Motors Research Laboratories.)

A dramatic full-color, shaded-surface display of a robot arm successfully imitates a photograph of an actual solid mechanism. (Courtesy of LogE/Dunn Instruments and Raster Technologies.)

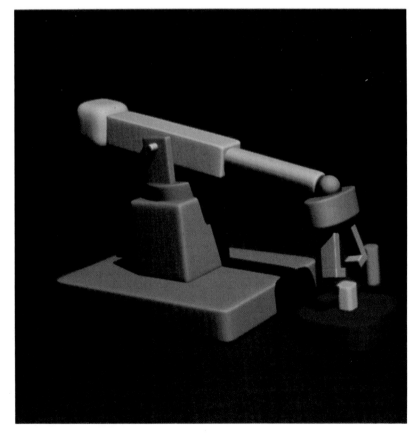

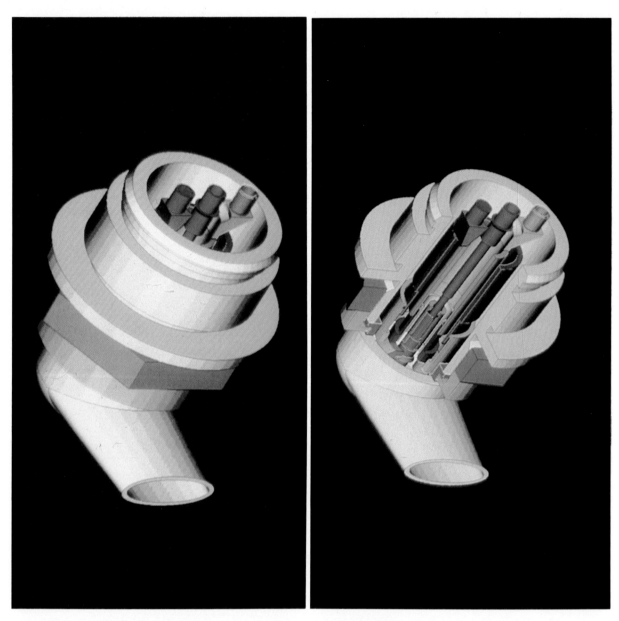

The approximation of curved shapes by a mesh of polygons is shown on the white and blue surfaces, which are supposed to be round. The number of polygons can be increased, with the size of each decreased, until the irregularity is invisible as in the Camaro model described on page 87. The lavender component has rectangular surfaces that are modeled, without distortion, by the polygon method. The technique of hidden-surface removal is also shown by the comparison of two images. **Left:** The covering obscures the internal detail, just as it would in a physical object. **Right:** A portion of the covering is cut away and the internal components are displayed from the computer model. In building this model the designer used a variety of colors to differentiate the closely packed components. (Courtesy of Aydin Controls.)

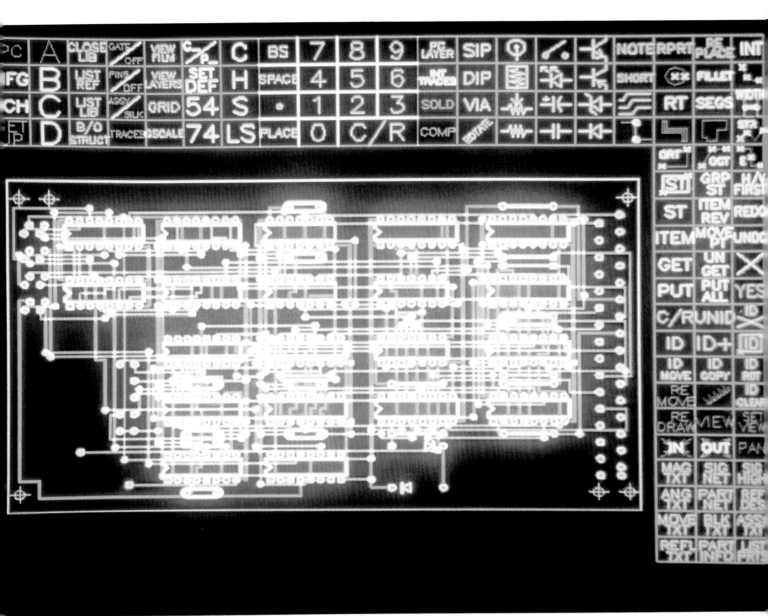

Color enhances the human interface of this graphics design system. Operations are controlled through the attractive screen menu at top and right. The remainder of the screen is devoted to the working design area, here displaying an overview of a printed circuit board layout. To effectively deal with a dense design, such as the one shown, the designer can take advantage of system options to zoom in for a magnified image of the area of interest and to display only selected logical layers, corresponding to specific color codes. (Courtesy of Calma Company, a wholly owned subsidiary of General Electric Company.)

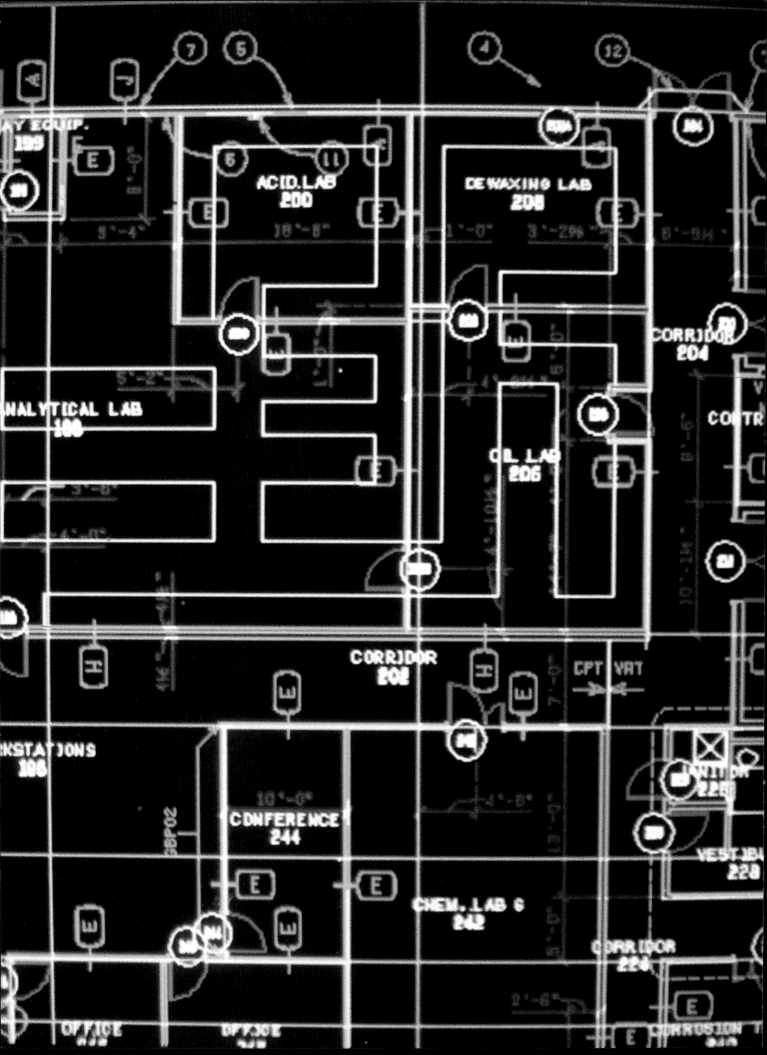

A design for an integrated circuit reveals that in electronics, as in commercial real estate development, the idea is to pack as many identical units onto as little property as possible, the property in electronics being a silicon chip. The symbol library in an interactive design system allows the designer to draw a symbol using line segments, store it under a name, and later call it forth and place it on a drawing whenever needed. One yellow square could be a symbol. Then a larger yellow rectangle is drawn, and sixteen of the previously defined yellow-square symbols are placed around it. The combination is then stored as a symbol in the library under a different name.

This is the concept of "nested symbols." When a combination with fourteen or with twenty, instead of sixteen, is needed, the combination symbol is placed, then modified. Larger portions of a design may also be copied from one area of a drawing to another without using the library. Rotated or mirrored copies are also easily placed. Repetition of symbols and patterns is inherently strong in integrated circuit design work, which is why huge productivity gains have been possible with computer graphics in electronics applications. (Reprinted with permission from Computervision Corporation, Bedford, MA.)

Opposite: This portion of a floor plan boldly demonstrates color discrimination of layers as a means of clarifying information on the screen. Two-dimensional drawings like this have shown a greater ratio of productivity improvement in the work of an architectural office than more dramatic three-dimensional renderings. (Courtesy of The Office of Pierce Goodwin Alexander.)

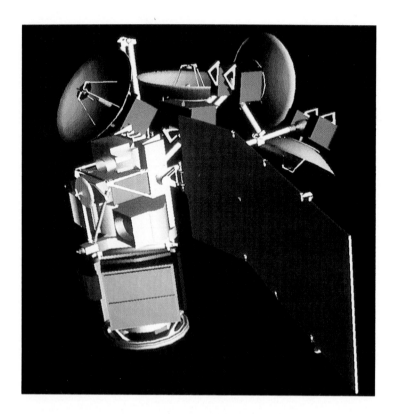

One stage of deployment for this satellite is shown in an image generated on a high-resolution screen. This solid modeling system is impressive in the degree of detail portrayed and in the realistic effects of lighting and shadows on the visible surfaces. Hidden surfaces are removed by the system when the image of the satellite, as seen from a specified point of view, is generated. (Courtesy of General Electric CAE International Inc.)

This Boeing 757, photographed from a display screen, is a computer model used for engineering simulations. (Courtesy of Evans & Sutherland and Rediffusion Simulation.)

Vibrant colors and a regular (but hardly monotonous) geometric pattern create the arresting visual impact of this scheme for an electronic circuit-board design. Although produced for practical purposes, the purely functional computer-generated graphic, suitably matted and framed, might otherwise serve well as a work of contemporary art. (Courtesy of Aydin Controls.)

4. IMAGINATION

Jim Garson

According to the popular view, computers are cold, dull and inflexible. They have nothing to do with creativity and imagination. This book should help prove that this idea is just a myth.

Computers have opened up new worlds for the artist. New techniques and visual styles are only beginning to be explored. Our culture is on the frontier of an era that will profoundly change the way art is produced and appreciated. Everyone has had some experience with these changes: compare the opening titles of television news programs ten years ago with those now. A whole new language of movement, color, shape, and special effects has been developed. The changes are liable to be even more spectacular in the next decade. Consider some of the more complex images in this book, imagine them in motion, and perhaps you will get just a hint of what to expect.

The Computer Artist's Toolbox: From Drawing to Programming

Because the computer allows so many special relationships between artists and their work, it is difficult to explain how computers are used to create art. For example, artists may work with the computer in a somewhat traditional manner, using a painting program with an electronic tablet and pen; or they may operate more like programmers, controlling their images by writing in a computer language at a keyboard. The versatility of the computer is exactly what makes

---

Opposite: *The astronomy of fascination. (Courtesy of LogE/Dunn Instruments and Gould DeAnza.)*

it so exciting. Artists can develop their own personal tools and methods for creating images. The same creativity which goes into visual expression can be used to define new relationships between the artist and the computer. Whole creative environments can be constructed in response to the artist's interests, talents, and tastes. Although each artist's approach to computer art is personal, we can still describe some of the major methods used to create the kind of work represented in this book.

Picture Systems: A Traditional Approach

Picture systems provide artists with tools that are similar to those found in their studios. The electronic pen and tablet simply replace pencil and paper. The pen is moved over the blank tablet, generating corresponding lines on a video screen, which creates an outline drawing. By pointing at color swatches in a palette displayed on the screen, the artist can mix his colors and then paint them into the outlines using the pen as a brush.

Although painting systems make no attempt to introduce radical methods, they offer a number of important advantages over traditional media. Working with ink, water-colors, or even oil can be heartbreaking. The slightest misstep can ruin a whole work. Even when no obvious error occurs, the artist may feel that the finished project needs a number of basic changes in color or shape which are impossible to carry out without ruining the work. Computerized painting systems are much more forgiving. They bring to graphics what word processors bring to writing. Artists can sketch and erase as much as they want without worrying about ruining a background.

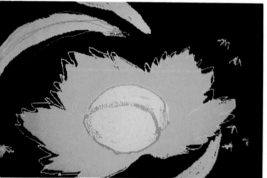

Two versions of a still-life in the modernist style, executed in the computer medium using the Paint System by Joseph S. Sipos, New York.

Not only are changes painless—the artist also has precise control over color and line. The paint never blobs, the colors never run, and the brush never needs cleaning. The computer can keep a perfect record of the artist's previous work. Such requests as "Give me the red color I used in last Sunday's sunset," can be quickly honored. Of course, some of the joy in mastering the craft is missing. But many artists will find that a price worth paying.

Novel Colors and Brushes

Picture systems often include useful features which are difficult to duplicate in handmade art. When the computer fills an outline with color, it is simply copying a color from the palette to another place on the video screen. It makes no difference to the computer whether the information copied looks like a solid color or a complex pattern. So it is a simple matter to let the artist fill his brush with a "color" which looks like a Scotch plaid or a tuft of green grass. A dress shape may be instantly filled with plaid, or the pen can be daubed over an area to create a field of hundreds of tufts of grass. One of the computer's strong points is its ability to repeat a process exactly. By letting the computer do the repetitive work, the artist is spared much of the tedious labor that is unavoidable with manual methods.

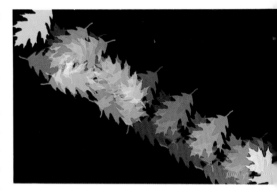

An electronic brush is dipped in colorful leaf shapes instead of paint to stroke this design by Carolyn Stapol, New York City. (Courtesy of Genigraphics Corp.)

In addition to complex colors and textures, some picture systems allow the artist to construct complex brushes. Airbrushes are popular devices because they create such subtle and perfectly graded shading. It is easy enough to provide the artist with a similar tool on the computer. A computerized airbrush simply adds tiny dots of color to the picture in a pattern similar to the cloud of spray of a real airbrush. On the computer, however, the artist has much better control over the shape the cloud will have, and he can easily change the color of the paint—*after* he has laid it down. He can even remove all the "airbrushed" color and start over.

Airbrushes are just one example of a whole array of special brushes which the artist may define. There are brushes which blend two colors at an edge or which change the color or texture of an area in subtle ways. Some artists even work with animated brushes, where whirling shapes leave fascinating circular patterns.

Orchids in bloom, drawn with a computer paint system. (Courtesy of J. K. Asch and Aydin Controls.)

Video Effects

Another approach to computerized art has its roots in television technology, and especially the techniques now used for advertisements and logos. The artist starts with a photograph, or handmade art, and stores it on the computer with a scanning camera. It can then be modified in many of the ways that are familiar from television. False colors can be assigned to parts of the picture, creating stunning and often confusing results. Pixelization is another popular technique: the smallest portions of a picture are averaged together into larger squares. The result is an image which is obviously composed of boxes of various shades but which still looks surprizingly like the original. There are a number of techniques for rotating, squashing, and distorting images. Im-

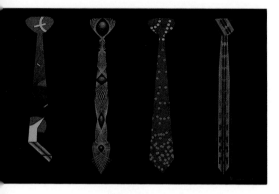

Ed Goes to Work *by Mike New-man, Dicomed Corporation.*

ages can even be "smeared" in interesting ways by moving the camera as the original is being scanned into the computer. Unique effects can be obtained without any original art at all, using video equipment to create electronic signals with distortion and feedback. In the past, most of these techniques were limited to very expensive special-purpose analog computers. But as digital computers have become more powerful, and the programming more sophisticated, many of these effects have become available on cheaper systems.

Creating Three-Dimensional Worlds

One of the most exciting areas of computer graphics research is the development of systems that let the user define three-dimensional objects on the computer and then display them on the screen. These systems are relatively expensive and are used in the design of buildings, cars, and aircraft (Chapter 3). There is still a long way to go before the images created on these systems are indistinguishable from the real thing. Even so, these three-dimensional systems are popular with some artists. Perhaps it is because the computer has the job of actually drawing the object on the screen. The artist defines the three-dimensional model of an object either by giving the positions of its edges or by building it up from a set of simple shapes. Once an object has been defined the artist can then look at it from any point of view to select an appealing image. One attraction is the "wire-frame" model of the object, which shows the edges but omits the surfaces, so that edges on the far side of an object are visible. By defining complex structures and looking at their wire-frame models from various points of view, beautiful spidery patterns can be created.

As graphics techniques improve, however, more attention is focused on the object's surfaces. Light, shadow, perspective, reflection, refraction, smoothing and texture are some of the most exciting and challenging areas of computer graphics research. The methods developed have greatly improved the appearance of computer-generated models and have provided the artist with a new vocabulary for visual expression.

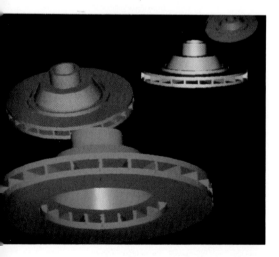

Whimsical use of solids modeling. (Courtesy of Lexidata.)

Experimentation with mathematical formulas for texture and light has produced surfaces with an appearance quite unlike anything we see in the real world. The brilliant highlights, glossiness, and luminous clouds which appear in television commercials are just some examples of special effects that owe their existence to computer graphics research.

Building three-dimensional objects with textured surfaces is a relatively difficult process, and displaying them makes enormous demands on the computer. Many of the more appealing tools are available only at a few research sites and any artist who uses them must be mathematically sophisticated. Nevertheless, the market for three-dimensional systems is growing quickly, and it should support the development of a whole new generation of computers that are relatively inexpensive and easy to use.

Skillful variation and repetition produced this intriguing pattern. (Courtesy of James A. Squires, Chromatics, Inc.)

Mathematical Creation

The techniques described so far have some connection with methods artists actually use; even three-dimensional modeling is something like sculpture. It is time to mention just a few of the effects that are unlike anything available in the artist's manual world. At present most of these techniques are understood only in a mathematical way and so are foreign and even frightening to many artists. But as these effects become more familiar, we are sure to find friendlier ways to use them.

Interpolation is probably the simplest of the mathematical methods to explain. Imagine an artist wants a sky that is perfectly shaded, from dark blue at the top to light blue at the horizon. Instead of painting, or even airbrushing it in, the artist has the computer do the job mathematically. All he needs to do is give the computer the shades at the top and the bottom of the sky. Since shades are represented as numbers, the computer can calculate the appropriate shade for each point on the screen depending on how near that point is to the top of the sky. For example, if the top shade is 100, and the bottom shade is 50, then a point which is exactly half way from the top should have shade 75 since that is exactly half the difference between the two shades.

The same idea can be applied to shape as well as color. Computers are now used to help in manufacturing cartoons. The animator draws a character in a beginning frame, and the same character in a later frame. The computer then calculates and draws the positions of the character in all the frames between them, saving an immense amount of labor. The same idea can be used in static art. By laying out a whole row of objects that gradually change shape from one thing to another, beautiful patterns can be created.

Interpolation can save the artist enormous effort and time, but there is another method that offers even more astonishing savings. Research into patterns found in nature has re-

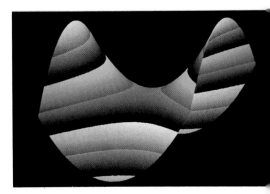

Color Saddle is the title of this software-generated sine function, produced by artist Jack Pines, Palo Alto, California. (Courtesy of Digital Graphic Systems, Inc.)

Softy: *A work of art generated mathematically through pixel-by-pixel interpolation of sine waves and tangents. (Courtesy of Frank Dietrich, West Coast University, Los Angeles.)*

Lake and Bird. *Talented use of color and technique create a sensitive image from a relatively low-resolution system designed primarily for videotext. (Courtesy of Jill Shargaa,* The Orlando Sentinel, Electronic Information Services.)

vealed mathematical formulas called *fractals* that describe structures which are "half way" between being totally random and completely orderly. The path of a shoreline, the surface texture of a mountain, and even patterns on fallen leaves all display this kind of order.

An artist who wants to create a landscape may avoid painting details by using fractals. He specifies the coefficients of a fractal formula, and the computer calculates and displays a semi-random structure which satisfies his formula. Once the artist has found a shoreline or mountain surface that pleases him, he may incorporate it into his work, creating a landscape that looks astonishingly real. At this point it is difficult to separate the artist's contribution to the work from the computer's.

This welding of the artist's and computer's contributions to the final work is characteristic of the more abstract mathematical approaches to computer art. The artist who works this way programs the computer to display mathematical formulas as patterns of color without necessarily having any idea of what the result will look like. As he experiments with the patterns which are formed, he acquires more knowledge about how his programs will behave, and eventually develops a brand new set of tools for creating images. It is very difficult to describe these efforts in any direct or detailed way. A whole new set of concepts is needed to communicate this properly. Perhaps the best thing to do is to abandon the effort to express these things verbally, and look at the pictures themselves.

What Computers Have Done to Artistic Style

Computer art is often associated with the kaleidoscopic spider web patterns which were so easy to produce on the equipment available in the 1960s. This book helps to demonstrate how artistic styles in computer art have developed since then. Although there is a much healthier variety in computer art, the methods and machinery used still have profound effects on how computer art looks today. Since most work is produced on a video screen, television has a strong effect on style. One of the most noticeable things about computer art is the color—color is emitted from a screen, not reflected from other light sources. It is bright, clear, flickery and luminescent. Dirty and calm colors are rarely seen, partly because they involve a complexity of tone and texture that takes effort to duplicate. Television is also a fairly low-resolution medium. You can easily see that the picture is made of tiny dots. The cheaper computer systems offer even less resolution, so that the boxes that form the image are apparent even at a casual glance. For the moment, we can expect computer art to be grainy, and for some artists to try to exploit this graininess in their work. Television advertisements have developed a special language of effects for the medium including highlights, fizz, fuzz, and fog. These visual clichés have had a strong effect on the way the television artist thinks about art.

It is difficult to predict where the style of computer art will go from here. Higher resolution will be available soon, but artists may wish to explore the low-resolution world somewhat longer. One thing though is certain: As systems and artists become more sophisticated a much more subtle and intricate world of visual expression will grow around us.

A scene from the main title sequence of the motion picture TRON © 1982 Walt Disney Productions. (Courtesy of Evans & Sutherland and Robert Abel and Associates.)

An autumn landscape in which the foliage is generated using a recursive tree-drawing algorithm. The program was written by artist Delle Maxwell, MIT Architecture Machine Group.

Waves propagate from a tower on a mesa in this abstract produced by the Abstractor program and CGC 7900 equipment. (Courtesy of James A. Squires, Chromatics, Inc.)

A Paris facade is recreated on the video screen by artist Rachel Gellman. This scene was drawn freehand on the "Video Palette 4" Paint System from Digital Effects, Inc., and converted from digital information to photographic slides on a Dicomed Film Recorder. (Courtesy of Rachel Gellman.)

This Cezanne-like still-life was "painted" by artist J. K. Asch using the Art Brush System, with Aycon-2000 hardware, and software created by T. Asch. (Courtesy of Aydin Controls.)

The Fractal Dragon, a graphic demonstration of a mathematical theory. Dr. Benoit Mandelbrot coined the word "fractal" from the Latin "fractus," meaning broken, to identify a new class of shapes: curves with infinite branching points. The intriguing thing about a fractal curve is that while the area inside the curve tends towards a finite value as the pattern gains greater detail, the length of the curve increases to infinity. Color was applied to the dragon-like shape by another computer algorithm. (Produced by Mark R. Laff and V. Alan Norton, IBM Research.)

Opposite: *Fractal Planetrise According to Mandelbrot,* a scene that exists only in the computer. In nature things are not identical at all magnifications. To model natural shapes more accurately, Dr. Mandelbrot introduces a random element into the calculations and produces extraordinarily convincing models of coastlines, rivers, mountains, lakes, islands, even the network of blood vessels in the lung. Different types of terrain can be generated on the computer's display screen by changing a few key variables in the mathematical equations. To enhance realism, color is added. (Produced by Richard Voss and Benoit Mandelbrot, IBM Research.)

The Fractal Dragon and *Fractal Planetrise* are copyright 1982 by Benoit B. Mandelbrot. Reprinted with permission from *The Fractal Geometry of Nature* by Benoit B. Mandelbrot, W. H. Freeman, 1982.)

Ed's Line Weave by Mike Newman, Dicomed Corporation. Free-form art work, created interactively at a design workstation, then photographed by a film recorder.

Eclipse in a confetti sky, created on Aurora's "paintbrush" system. (Courtesy of Gould DeAnza.)

Opposite: Artist Joanne P. Culver produced *Magic City* on special graphics equipment developed by Bally-Midway Mfg., Inc., with programming written in ASSEMBLER.

Scenes from the history and mythology of various cultures are built with "nested symbols." For instance, in the second image a small pattern is repeated vertically to design a column, then columns are repeated with gradual reduction to create the illusion of depth. ©1982 CBS, Inc. Artist: Mark Zweigler. **From top left:** *Oriental Palace, Taj Mahal, Mummy's Tomb, Inferno City, Ancient Ruin,* and *Russian Palace.*

Mondo Condo, by Ned Greene. This scene was composed in preparation for an animation sequence which will show movement through a structure from the point of view of a walking robot. To render the scene it was necessary to create a three-dimensional geometric description of the environment from primitive surfaces. The architectural structure was modeled from roughly 10,000 polygons and each of the robots consists of about 200 "quadric surfaces"—ellipsoids, cylinders, hyperboloids, etc. The terrain in the background was represented as a fine mesh of polygons, its features specified by a program that created random fluctuations in shape. (Courtesy of Ned Greene, New York Institute of Technology Computer Graphics Laboratory.)

Pt. Reyes. This extremely sophisticated computer landscape was defined using patches, polygons, fractals, particle systems, and a variety of proce-dural models. The various elements were rendered separately and later composited. (Courtesy of Alvy Ray Smith, Lucasfilm Ltd.)

White Sands. The flowering plants were grown in three dimensions from a single cell using an algorithmic computer model, and the grasses were drawn using a procedural modeling technique. (Courtesy of Alvy Ray Smith, Lucasfilm Ltd.)

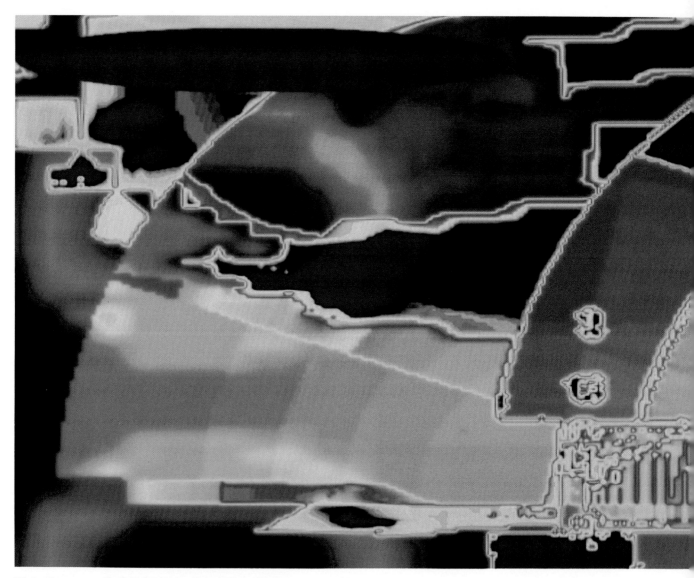

This abstract called *Sahara.2* is by artist J. Michael O'Rourke of the New York Institute of Technology (NYIT). The design was produced using NYIT software, a DEC VAX 11/780 computer, Genisco frame buffers, and a Dicomed D48 film recorder.

The soft, neutral colors of nature appear in the works of two artists who apply the capabilities of a business graphics system to fine art. **Top:** *Mexico,* by Sharon Hendry, Houston. **Bottom:** *Wheat,* by Brenda Davidson, Houston. (Both images courtesy of Genigraphics Corporation.)

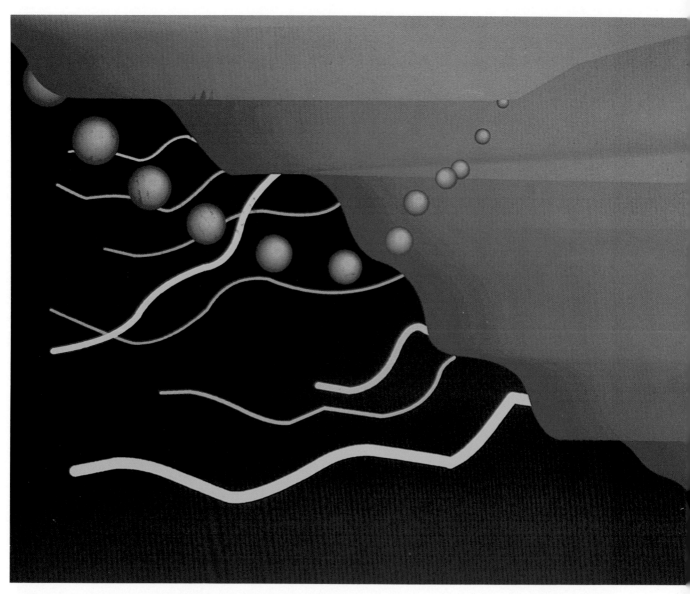

Ed's Snake Dream by Mike Newman, Dicomed Corporation.

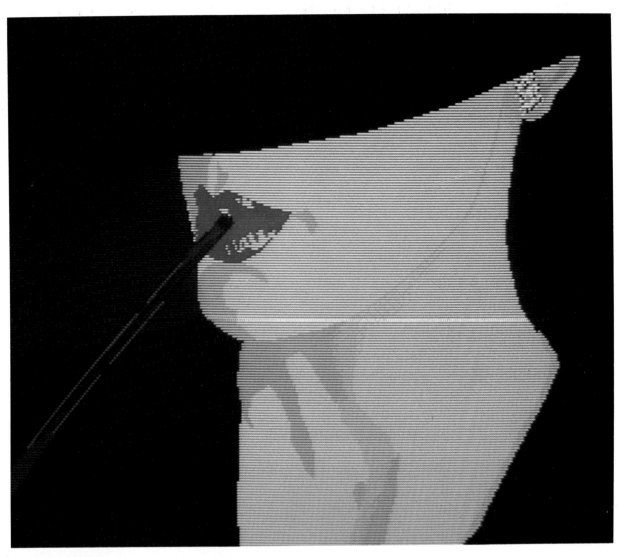

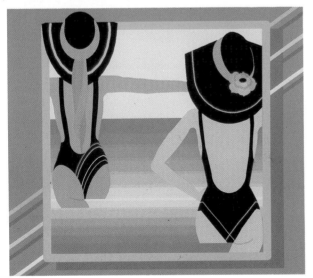

The slick, commercial look produced by computer systems dedicated to presentation graphics is used to advantage in these portraits of women. **Above:** Artwork by the Hemton Group, a Division of NORPAK Corporation, Ontario, Canada, using a videotext frame-creation system called the IPS-2. The jagged edges of curves are the result of the limited resolution available in the videotext protocol, designed for efficient transmission over telecommunication channels.

Left: Scene by Patricia M. Earley at Genigraphics Corporation, Houston, working at a Series 100 Console. The extremely high resolution of this 35mm slide-production system makes curves look smooth.

The images on this page illustrate three-dimensional Beta-spline interpolation, a curve-fitting technique made possible with computer graphics. In earlier times when a draftsman needed to find a curve that passed through or near a set of given points, he located weights at the data points and then placed a flexible wood or metal strip (a spline) against the weights to obtain a smooth curve. Curve-fitting problems occur in industrial design and manufacturing, as well as in graphics research. (Courtesy of Brian A. Barsky, Tony D. DeRose, and Mark D. Dippé, Berkeley Computer Graphics Laboratory, University of California.)

An array of three different Beta-spline objects with tension increasing from left to right and bias fixed. The objects increase in complexity from top to bottom. They are constructed from various simulated glossy materials, including metallic and plastic substances.

This array is based on a single, shiny, textured Beta-spline bottle. Both the tension and bias are varied. The tension increases from left to right and the bias increases from top to bottom.

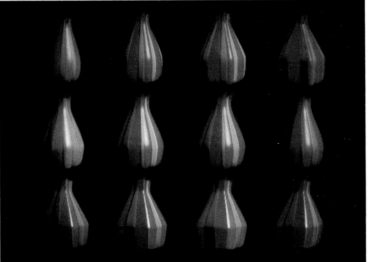

Variations derived from a single Beta-spline bottle with the tension increasing from left to right and from top to bottom in an exponential fashion. The bias remains fixed throughout. Each of the bottles has different material characteristics including metallic, dusty, and plastic substances.

The crystal sphere in the foreground is a simulated transparent object. All three large spheres have a texture applied to their surfaces. The opaque ones have color (even a photograph!) applied over the surface texture. The highlights reflected by the spheres, and the shadow cast by the smallest one, are simulated lighting effects. This demonstration scene was produced with experimental ray-tracing software. (Courtesy of Peter Watterberg, Sandia National Laboratories.)

A camera's blurred depth-of-field lens effect is simulated by software that can reproduce an image according to the laws of optics (left side). When the special optical effect is not used (right side), a sharp mathematically defined image is produced. Done by Michael Potmesil at Rensselaer Polytechnic Institute. (Courtesy of Gould DeAnza.)

This solid model of a locomotive was created for use in an animated movie. It was computed on a Control Data Corporation CYBER using SynthaVision software, the same solid-modeling software used to design the crankshaft shown on page 80. This multi-purpose software is indeed flexible in the hands of an imaginative user. The image was photographed using a Matrix 4007 color hardcopy unit. (Produced by Bill Charlesworth and Dave Plunkett at the Purdue CADLAB. Courtesy of Michael J. Bailey, Purdue University.)

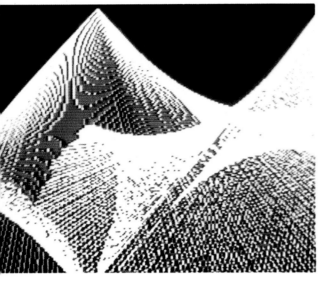
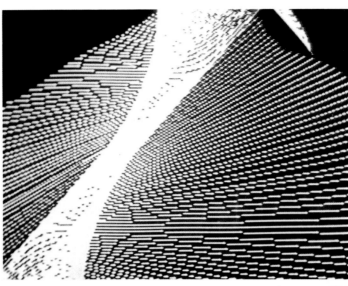

A series of patterns produced by a "slowly rotating brush" drawing on the screen of an Apple II personal computer under the control of a program written in PASCAL by the artist. The image increases in complexity as the computer carries out an iterative mathematical formula. (Courtesy of James W. Garson, University of Houston.)

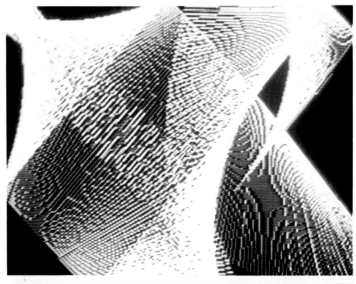

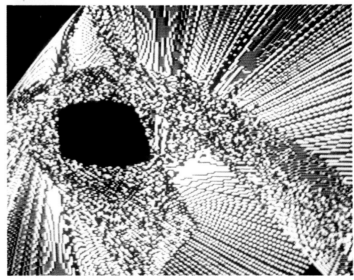

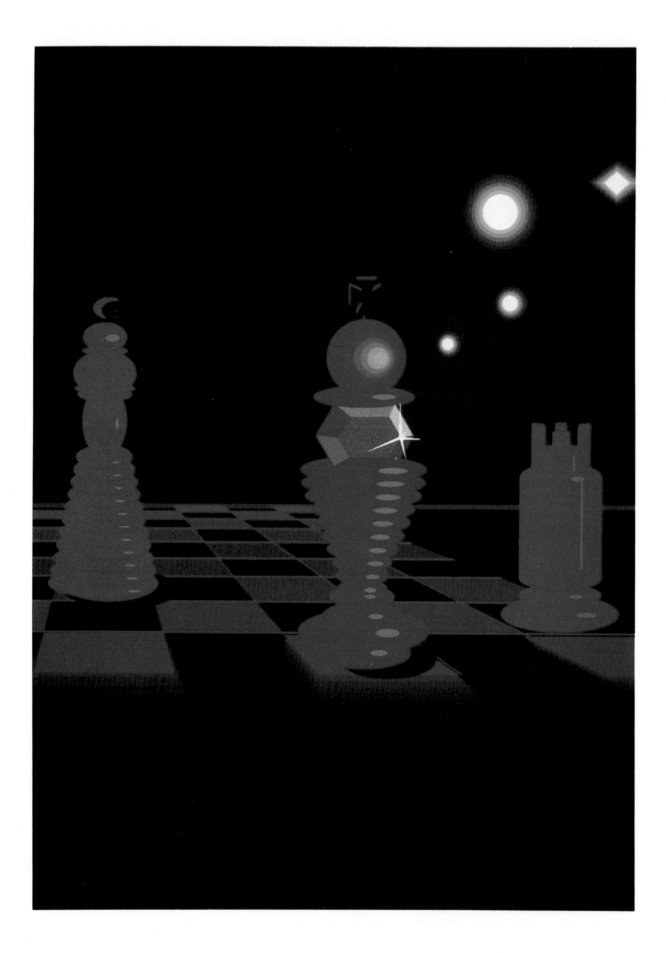

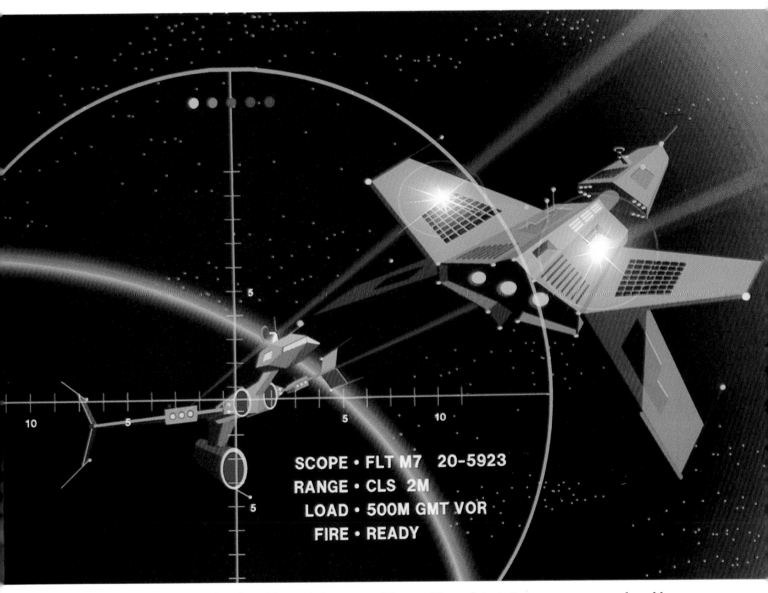

SCOPE • FLT M7 20-5923
RANGE • CLS 2M
LOAD • 500M GMT VOR
FIRE • READY

A science-fiction battle, fought with exotic beams and forces. These futuristic images were produced by Jim Rabon, Atlanta. (Courtesy of the Genigraphics Corporation.)

Opposite: An interstellar chess game, played in dramatic red and blue. Artist: Jim Rabon, Atlanta. (Courtesy of the Genigraphics Corporation.)

An evocative image by artist Kazuo Morita, Hoei Sangyo, Ltd. Tokyo. (Courtesy of Aurora Systems.)

Night Castles, by Ned Greene. The castle was modeled in three dimensions, each tower consisting of about 1900 polygons. The reflection was created by rendering the model upside down across the plane of the water and blurring the result. Water was simulated by texture mapping a wave pattern onto a single polygon, and the sky was manually painted with an interactive paint program. (Courtesy of Ned Greene, New York Institute of Technology Computer Graphics Laboratory.)

Zlik (**opposite**) and *Dr. Jim Number 1* (**above**) were generated while David Em was artist-in-residence at the Jet Propulsion Laboratory, using software developed by Dr. Jim Blinn. The graphics programs were designed to create motion-picture simulations of deep-space phenomena for NASA. (See pages 10 and 11.) Em adapted the computer system to his artistic purposes, but he acknowledges that the astrophysics environment unconsciously influenced his aesthetics.

David Em's *Gabriel* (**above**), *Dream* (**top right**) and *Maya* (**bottom right**) were created using an integrated graphics system consisting of four basic kinds of programs. A paint program and two-dimensional transformation program allow the creation of intricate patterns with great efficiency. A three-dimensional program enables the artist to synthesize solid shapes, apply the pattern to their surfaces, and display them realistically. Finally, an animation program uses the results of the other programs to generate a film or video-tape.

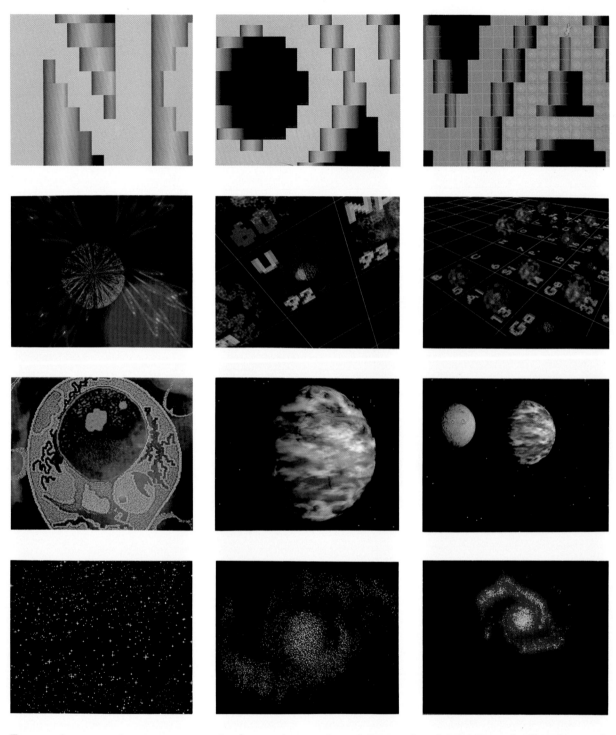

From microcosm to macrocosm. A change in scale that takes the viewer from the atomic to the cosmic is compressed into this 15-second animated opening sequence for the television series *NOVA,* produced for WGBH, Boston. (View the sequence from top left across both pages.) Production required coordination of diverse computer animation techniques, from highly sophisticated interactive "artist-intensive" tasks—such as painting with an electronic palette—to tasks requiring complex mathematical modeling and great amounts of digital processing. Graphic designer: Paul Souza. Director/animator: David M. Geshwind. Facility: New York Institute of Technology. (Courtesy of David M. Geshwind, Digital Video Systems.)

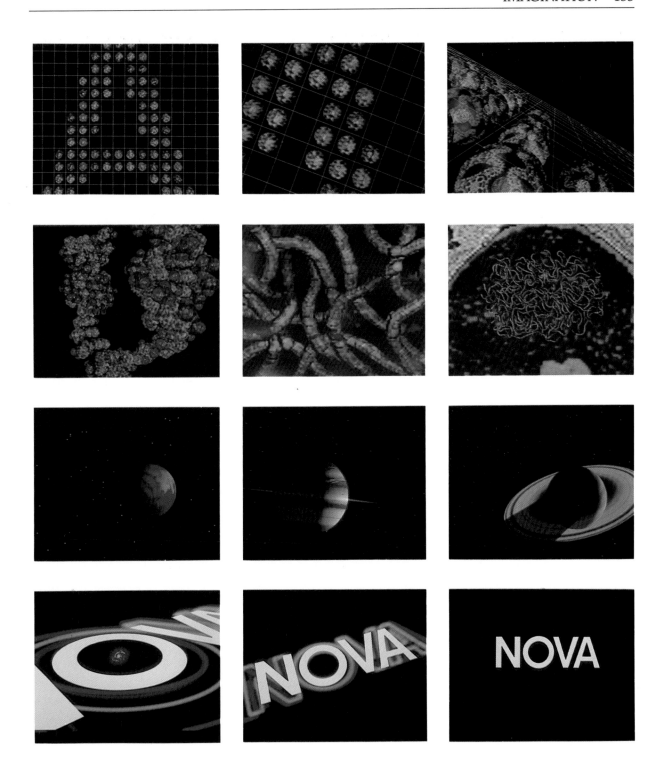

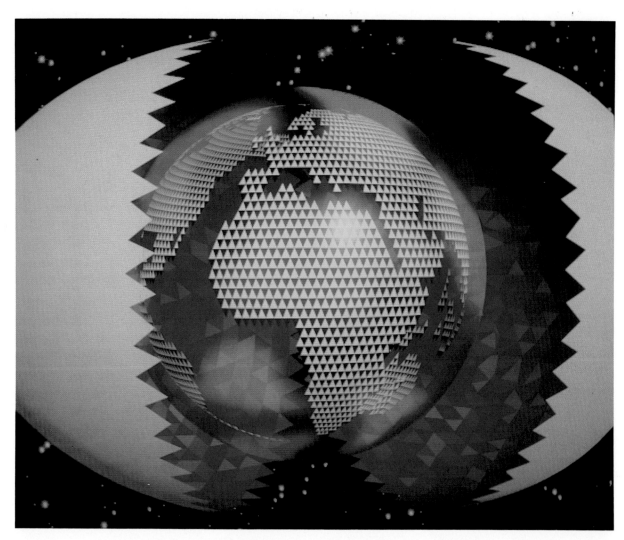

Rebirth, a three-dimensional egg, opening to reveal a globe, rendered as a multiplicity of polygons with CCP software on a DEC VAX 11/780 computer with a 640 x 484 x 32-bit frame buffer. Animator: Michael T. Collery. (Courtesy of Cranston-Csuri Productions, Inc.)

Ray-tracing spheres simulate light refraction and shadow in *Algorithmic Dream*. This image represents advanced techniques in computer graphics display generation. Animators: Shaun Ho and Michael Collery. (Courtesy of Cranston-Csuri Productions, Inc.)

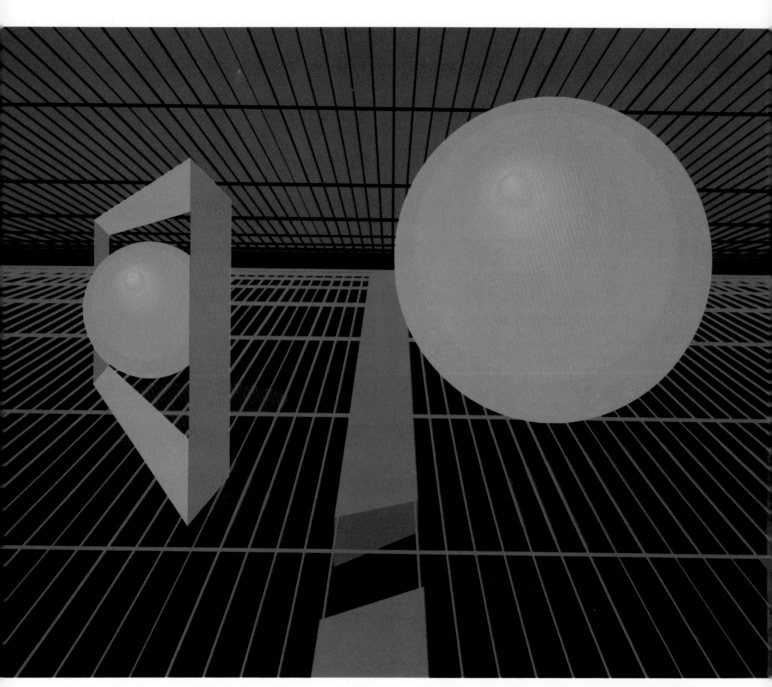

Floating shapes in a gridded perspective. The highlight and shadow effects of a pretended light source are produced with a commercial art graphics system. The shadows are offset copies of the basic shapes. The highlights are circles of lighter shades, complimented by a gradient of shades in circles out to a darker edge. The perspective effect is done with a computer-calculated compression of the background design. Drawn by Tony Casadonte, Miami. (Courtesy of Genigraphics Corporation.)

Opposite: *Dive* was produced on a Digital Equipment PDP-1145 with a Vector General Display and video image-processed with the Sandin Image Processor. (Courtesy of the artist, Joanne P. Culver.)

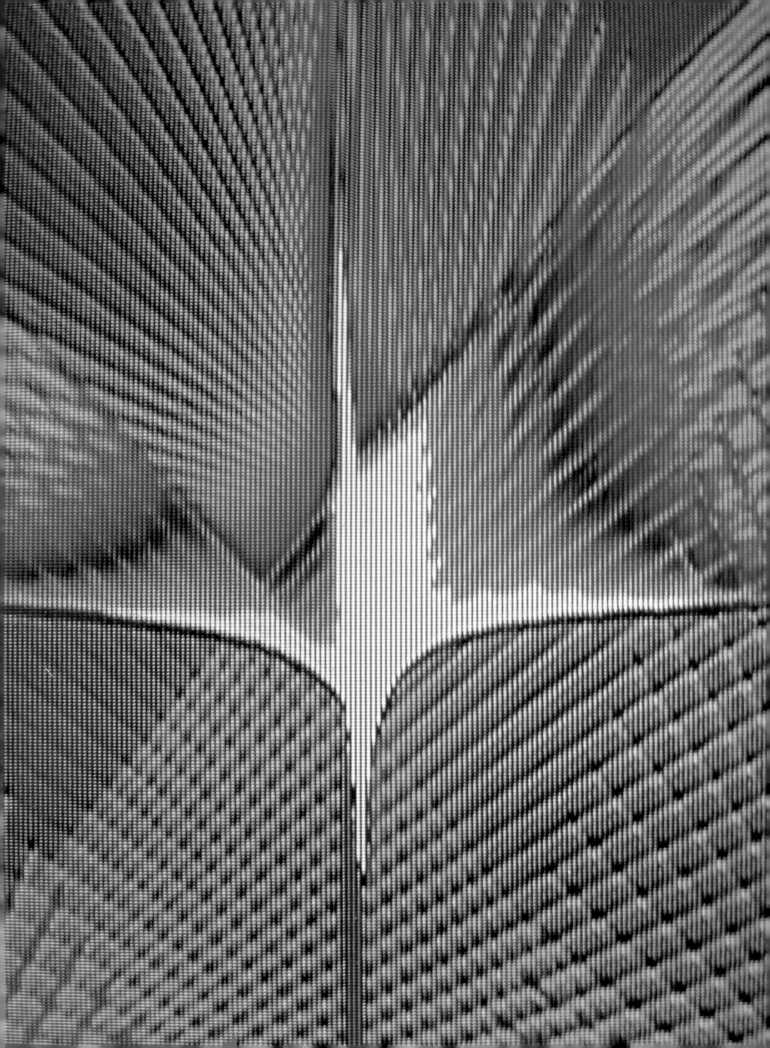

Into by Joanne P. Culver was an award-winner in an international exhibition of computer graphics art.

Multiple Suns (close-up) by Joanne P. Culver.

Electronic metamorphosis: One picture dissolves into another in these three frames from an animated sequence. The color and line values are identical in all three images—they have simply been rearranged on the screen by the computer. (Courtesy of Computer Creations, South Bend, IN.)

Wire frame ovoids float from a base of blue **(below)** through a carousel of orange polyhedra **(above).** (Courtesy of Delle Maxwell, MIT Visible Language Workshop.)

A landscape of grids and polyhedra. (Courtesy of Delle Maxwell, MIT Visible Language Workshop.)

A series of mathematical transformations built the geometry in this design. (Courtesy of Delle Maxwell, MIT Architectural Machine Group.)

This stylized drawing of a mountain at sunset was composed with a Beacon 610 color graphics computer using IBIS Illustration System software. Stunning visual effects like these can be achieved by alternating shadows with light. (Courtesy of Eleanor Matthews, Fairfield Graphics Division, Florida Computer Graphics, Seattle.)

Launch pad at dawn, a detailed fantasy vision by Jim Rabon, Atlanta. (Courtesy of Genigraphics Corporation.)

GLOSSARY

Elizabeth Patton

Algorithm—A collection of mathematical steps for the completion of a single task.

Analog Computer—A computer that represents information in voltages instead of digits. See digital computer.

Animation—The illusion of motion created by successive pictures of inanimate objects with slight position change.

Bandwidth—The range of a frequency or color.

Bit Plane—A two-dimensional matrix representing the pixels of a graphic monitor.

Cathode Ray Tube (CRT)—Commonly refers to a fluorescent screen used to display computer information. The screen is illuminated by electron beams.

Central Processing Unit (CPU)—The central calculating unit of a computer.

Clipping—The process of eliminating the part of a picture that is outside the viewing frame.

Color Scale—The table of color descriptions using any method of color definition.

Computer-Aided Design (CAD)—The process of creating or modifying a design via computer.

Computer-Aided Manufacturing (CAM)—The process of controlling the operations of a manufacturing plant via a computer.

Computer Graphics—The area of computer technology providing a final output of a picture or a series of pictures.

Contours—A set of lines connecting like values of a set of data.

Coordinates—The system of x, y and (for three-dimensional modeling) z axes that are defined for a particular application. The database is built in "world" coordinates and the image is displayed in "device" coordinates.

Cursor—A visible symbol, often flashing, which marks the active control point.

DAC—Digital to analog converter. Converts discrete data to continuous.

Data—Numerical values.

Database—A collection of data organized such that any set or subset of it is easily retrievable.

Device Independent—Software that is written in modular form so that the main application program is not tied to particular graphics peripherals. Instead, small "device-driver" programs handle communications with input and output devices.

Digital Computer—A computer that deals with numbers as digits.

Digitize—The process of mechanically tracing a picture and converting it to numerical codes the computer can recognize.

Direct View Storage Tube (DVST)—A display device that uses electron beams to excite long persistence phosphors so as to keep a display on the screen without refreshing.

Electrostatic Plotter—An output device that uses a raster of electrically charged particles to apply an image to paper.

Film Recorder—An output device that uses a high-resolution monochrome CRT and color filter wheels to record an image on photographic film.

Flicker—An irritating flashing of the image on the screen due to insufficient refresh rate.

Frame buffer—A memory array used to store the numerical data for displaying a complete image.

Geodesy—The geologic science of the shape and size of the earth.

Graphical Kernel System (GKS)—Standard for graphics systems designed by the International Standards Organization.

Graphic Primitives—The simplest elements of a picture which could consist of points, lines, circles, or arcs.

Gridding—The procedure of calculating even incremental values from a collection of random points. The result is an evenly spaced matrix of interpolated values.

Hardware—The physical machinery, such as the computer or graphics terminal.

Hard Copy—A physical copy of the desired image on paper, film or any other media.

Hidden-line Removal—Computer techniques that determine which lines in a wire frame image are not visible from a particular viewpoint and which remove them from the displayed image.

Hidden-surface Removal—Computer techniques that determine which surfaces in a solid model (or surface model) are not visible from a particular viewpoint and which remove them from the displayed image.

Hologram—A photograph of a three-dimensional image created by wavefront reconstruction using lasers.

Image Processing—The analysis of scenes utilizing tools such as pattern recognition and image enhancements.

Interlaced—Referring to refreshing an image on the screen. The odd numbered scan lines are refreshed, then the even numbered scan lines.

Interpolation—Given beginning and ending points, calculating the internal points along a smooth gradient.

Ink-jet Plotter—An output device that squirts tiny amounts of ink in specified locations (all under computer control) to create color graphics images.

Iterative (iteration)—A calculation that is repeated many times with slight variation designated for each repetition.

Jaggies—The uneven appearance of diagonal lines in a matrix of pixels on low-resolution graphics output devices.

Landsat—Multi-spectrum pictures of the earth's surface taken from a satellite.

Mapping—Changing data from one format to another without alteration.

Matrix—Numbers arranged in rows and columns, which are particularly suitable as a format for programming graphics transformations.

Menu—A list or matrix of available graphics commands, usually appearing on the screen or on a digitizer.

Microprocessor—One chip or integrated circuit that contains an entire central processing unit (CPU).

Molecular Modeling—A tool used by chemists to build three-dimensional models of molecules based on limited information concerning their physical attributes.

Monitor—Display device in a graphics system, usually a CRT.

Numerical Control (NC)—Computerized control of machine tools, used in the manufacturing industry.

Picture/Painting Systems—A hardware and software system used by artists allowing the user to treat the computer and its peripherals as an easel, paintbrush and palette.

Palette—The array of colors available to the artist/designer.

Pen Plotter—A plotting device that can interpret computer instructions into physical motion of a pen onto paper or other presentation media.

Perspective—To represent on a flat surface the relationship of objects in space as they might appear in a three-dimensional world.

Pixel—One dot or picture element of the screen of a raster CRT.

Pixelization—Averaging pixels into larger squares.

Polygon—A two-dimensional closed figure bounded by straight lines.

Polyhedron—A solid figure having plane faces.

Primary Colors—The palette of colors needed to create all other colors. Each primary color cannot be created from any other color.

Procedures—The instructions for performing certain operations on data, distinct from the various data sets to which the procedures are applied.

Pseudo-color—Color attribute given an image or part of an image due to the data value, not to its actual real-world representation.

Raster—A rectangular array of dots or points.

Rectilinear Scanner—A digital scanner that breaks an object into horizontal lines and records it as such.

Reflection—The idea of mirroring an image. Also, the reflection of light bouncing off a surface.

Refraction—The apparent displacement of an object due to light rays passing through a variety of media.

Refresh—To redraw an image on the screen either interlaced or noninterlaced rapidly enough to keep it viewable before phosphor decay.

Resolution—A measure of the fineness of detail in an image. For raster devices, the number of dots in a defined area. For vector devices, the number of lines in a defined area.

Rotation—Turning an image in two or three dimensions.

Simulation—The representation of a device or capability through the creative use of another device or capability. Also, the representation of an object or process by a computer model.

Scale Factor—The ratio used to change something from one size to another.

Scan Line—One horizontal line of dots or pixels. The unit used for refresh.

Scanning Camera—A camera that has the ability to read an image one horizontal line at a time.

Shaded-surface Model—An object showing the surfaces as opaque planes, a display technique that produces extremely realistic results.

Smoothing—Averaging a surface to eliminate irregularities and roughness.

Software—The set of instructions given to the computer in the form of programs.

Solid Modeling—Objects defined by volumes. Examples: spheres, cones, polyhedra, and complex combinations of these figures.

Surface Modeling—Representing a complex shape as if a cloth were draped over the datapoints. A surface is three-dimensional but does not have any volume. (See Solid Modeling.)

Texture—Three-dimensional relief of a surface.

Transformation—Any mathematical operation to change stored data.

Translation—Moving an image with respect to the coordinate system.

Turnkey System—Computer hardware and instructions integrated to complete a specific task or application, sold to the user as an integrated system.

Vector—A straight line defined by a starting point and an ending point.

Video Lookup Table—A table of color definitions.

Videotext (Also Videotex, Viewdata)—Pictures and text such as newspapers, shopping catalogs and stock quotes transmitted over broadcast television or telephone for interaction by home viewers.

View Point—The position of the eyeball of the viewer for proper perspective.

Window—The portion of the image in the database that is to be viewed. The window is mapped to the viewport.

Wire Frame Model—An object showing all the edges of the polygons, but omitting the surfaces so that the viewer can see through the picture. A short-cut display technique.

Workstation—A combination of graphics input and output devices, usually with local intelligence (i.e., a microprocessor).

ABOUT THE CONTRIBUTORS

Allen Buford is Region Computer Engineer for the Gulf Coast Area of Cities Service Oil and Gas. His experience has been related to computer graphics for seismic data interpretation and to programming of supervisory control and data acquisition (SCADA) systems, used for pipeline and utility control applications. He graduated from the University of Houston with a B.S. in Computer Science and is a member of Third Coast Computer Graphics Group, the IEEE Computer Society, The Association for Computing Machinery's Special Interest Group on Graphics (ACM/SIGGRAPH), ACM/SIGART (artificial intelligence), and ACM/SIGBIO (biomedicine computer applications). His position as president of the Houston Chapter of the National Hemophilia Foundation has lead him to establish extensive contacts within the local medical community, which proved valuable in gathering information for the LIFE introduction.

Scot Carpenter is Assistant Professor in the College of Technology, University of Houston, where he teaches courses in computer-aided design and drafting (CADD). His research interests include CADD applications in manufacturing and construction, microcomputer applications for CADD, curriculum for CADD, and integrated data bases for engineering applications. He was previously an engineer/analyst for Synercom Technology, Inc., a major CADD-system vendor. His academic background includes a B.S. in Industrial Education and an M.S. in Industrial Technology, both from Texas A&M University. Mr. Carpenter's professional memberships are Phi Kappa Phi, Society of Manufacturing Engineers-CASA, IEEE Computer Society, ACM/SIGGRAPH, and he is immediate past president of the Third Coast Computer Graphics Group.

James W. Garson is associate professor in the Department of Philosophy, University of Houston. His research interests include logic, natural language processing, computer languages, and computers in education. He has taught computer graphics at the Computer Science Department of the University of Illinois, Chicago Circle, where he was also director of the Electronics Visualization Laboratory, which is devoted to the development of graphics systems for artists and educators. Dr. Garson has held a number of grants involving applications of computer graphics to education, and has published several articles on this topic. He earned his Ph.D. in Philosophy at the University of Pittsburgh. His memberships in computer-related professional societies include IEEE, ACM/

SIGGRAPH (graphics), ACM/SIGART (artificial intelligence), ACM/ SIGCUE (computer uses in education). Dr. Garson is the current president of the Third Coast Computer Graphics Group.

Jonathan S. Linowes is a degree candidate for the M.S. in Visual Studies at the Massachusetts Institute of Technology, where he is also engaged as a research assistant in the Visible Language Workshop, Arts and Media Technology Laboratory. His interests include intelligent user interfaces, graphic design methodologies, software design, artificial intelligence, and expert systems. He holds a B.A. in Fine Arts from Syracuse University, where he pursued a self-designed concentration in computer graphics and film.

He joined the Third Coast Computer Graphics Group while in Houston working for Texas Instruments as a graphics software and systems engineer in future products research and development. He currently serves as a software design consultant to several firms. Mr. Linowes' professional affiliations also include American Association of Artificial Intelligence, ACM/SIGGRAPH, SIGPLAN, SIGSOFT, Boston Computer Society and the IEEE Computer Society.

Elizabeth Patton of Houston, Texas is a Systems Engineer with Lexidata Corporation, a computer graphics hardware firm. She has had extensive experience in graphics programming for energy-related applications, such as developing database acquisition tools and display routines for a seismic interpretation system, and designing programs for digitizer input, previewing, and editing of well log data and horizons. She also has worked as a system analyst for Tektronix, a leading vendor of graphics display devices. Ms. Patton holds a B.S. in Mathematics from the University of Houston and is a member of the Third Coast Computer Graphics Group.

Joan E. Scott is president of Scott Consulting Services, Houston, Texas. She was previously coordinator of computer-aided drafting and design for Fluor Engineers. Her special interest is the application of computer graphics in process plant design and construction. She holds a B.A. degree from Rice University. Mrs. Scott is listed in *Marquis Who's Who Directory of Computer Graphics* and is a member of the National Computer Graphics Association (NCGA), the IEEE Computer Society, ACM/SIGGRAPH, and is treasurer of the Third Coast Computer Graphics Group. Mrs. Scott is the author of *Introduction to Interactive Computer Graphics* published by Wiley-Interscience.

Richard W. Verm is co-director of the Cullen Image Processing Laboratory, one of the University of Houston's Allied Geophysical Laboratories, a group of industry-sponsored laboratories engaged in petroleum exploration research. The image processing lab is active in applying interactive computer graphics to this area, in particular to computer-aided seismic interpretation and three-dimensional displays of seismic data. Dr. Verm received his B.A. from Rice University and his M.S. and Ph.D. from the Department of Geosciences, University of Houston. He is a member of the Society of Exploration Geophysicists (SEG), ACM/SIGGRAPH, and the Third Coast Computer Graphics Group.

SOURCES

Editor's note:

The companies, institutions, and individuals listed here were the direct contacts for the images contributed to this book. In some cases, others supplied the images to these contacts, as noted in the captions to the photographs.

Abel, Robert & Associates
953 North Highland
Hollywood, CA 90038

Applicon, A Schlumberger
Company
32 Second Avenue
Burlington, MA 01803

Aurora Systems
185 Berry Street, Suite 143
San Francisco, CA 94107

Aydin Controls
414 Commerce Drive
Fort Washington, PA 19034

Berkeley Computer Graphics
Laboratory
Computer Science Division
University of California
Berkeley, CA 94720

Boeing Aerospace Company
P.O. Box 3999
Seattle, WA 98124

Brown University
Providence, RI 02912

Calma Company
2901 Tasman Drive
Santa Clara, CA 95050

Cities Service Oil and Gas
P.O. Box 300
Tulsa, OK 74102

Computer Creations
1657 N. Commerce Drive, Suite 1B
South Bend, IN 46628

Comtal/3M
505 West Woodbury Road
Altadena, CA 91001

Computervision Corporation
100 Crosby Drive
Bedford, MA 01730

Contour Medical Systems, Inc.
1931-A Old Middlefield Way
Mountain View, CA 94043

Control Data Corporation
8100 34th Avenue South
Minneapolis, MN 55440

Cranston-Csuri Productions, Inc.
1501 Neil Avenue
Columbus, OH 43201

Culver, Joanne P.
633 N. 13th
DeKalb, IL 60115

Dicomed Corporation
9700 Newton Avenue South
Minneapolis, MN 55431

Dietrich, Frank
West Coast University
440 Shatto Place
Los Angeles, CA 90020

Digital Graphic Systems, Inc.
935 Industrial Avenue
Palo Alto, CA 94303

Digital Video Systems, Inc.
111 Fourth Avenue
New York, NY 10003

Em, David
c/o James Seligman
183 South Detroit
Los Angeles, CA 90036

Evans & Sutherland
580 Arapeen Drive
Salt Lake City, UT 84108

Fairfield Graphics Division
Florida Computer Graphics
1923 1st Avenue, Suite 300
Seattle, WA 98101

Gellman, Rachel
192 Bleecker Street #21
New York, NY 10012

General Electric CAE
International, Inc.
300 TechneCenter Drive
Milford, OH 45150

General Motors Research
Laboratories
David R. Warn, Computer Science
Department
Warren, MI 48090

Genigraphics Corporation
4806 W. Taft Rd.
Liverpool, NY 13088

Geosource, Inc.
6909 Southwest Freeway
Houston, TX 77074

Gerber Systems Technology, Inc.
40 Gerber Road East
South Windsor, CT 06074

Gould Inc.
DeAnza Imaging &
   Graphics Division
1870 Lundy Avenue
San Jose, CA 95131

Hermann Hospital
1203 Ross Sterling Avenue
Houston, TX 77030

Hershey Medical Center
The Pennsylvania State University
Hershey, Pennsylvania 17033

Intergraph Corporation
1 Madison Industrial Park
Huntsville, AL 35807

Jet Propulsion Laboratory
California Institute of Technology
4800 Oak Grove Drive
Pasadena, CA 91109

Lexidata
755 Middlesex Turnpike
Billerica, MA 01865

LogE/Dunn Instruments, Inc.
544 2nd Street
San Francisco, CA 94107

Lucasfilm Ltd.
P.O. Box 2009
San Rafael, CA 94912

Mallinckrodt Institute
Washington University School
   of Medicine
510 S. Kings Highway
St. Louis, MO 63110

Mandelbrot, Dr. Benoit B.
IBM Research Center
P.O. Box 218
Yorktown Heights, NY 10598

Maxwell, Delle
12 Sunset Road
West Somerville, MA 02144

Merck Sharp & Dohme Research
   Laboratories
Merck and Co., Inc.
P.O. Box 2000
Rahway, NJ 07065

Molnar, Zsuzsanna
Silicon Graphics
630 Clyde Court
Mountain View, CA 94043

National Oceanic and
   Atmospheric Administration
Environmental Research
   Laboratories
325 Broadway
Boulder, CO 80303

Nelson, Douglas
Sun Star Productions
31155 Lobo Vista
Agoura, CA 91301

New York Institute of Technology
P.O. Box 170
Old Westbury, NY 11568

NORPAK Corporation
10 Hearst Way
Kanata, Ontario, Canada K2L 2P4

Optronics International, Inc.
7 Stuart Road
Chelmsford, MA 01824

Orlando Sentinel, The
Electronic Information Services
633 North Orange Avenue
Orlando, FL 32801

Oxford University
Laboratory of Molecular Biophysics
South Parks Road
Oxford, England OX1 3PS

Phoenix Computer Graphics
1309 Pinhook Road
Lafayette, LA 70505

Pierce Goodwin Alexander,
   The Office of
800 Bering Drive
Houston, TX 77057

Purdue University
CADLAB, Potter Engineering
   Center
West Lafayette, IN 47907

Rice University
P.O. Box 1892
Houston, TX 77251

St. Luke's Episcopal and
   Texas Children's Hospitals
   and the Texas Heart Institute
6621 Fannin
Houston, TX 77030

Sandia National Laboratories
P.O. Box 5800
Albuquerque, NM 87185

Scripps Clinic and Research
   Foundation
10666 North Torrey Pines Road
La Jolla, CA 92037

SEDIC
Seibu Digital Communications, Inc.
Digital Graphic Studio
Wave Bldg. 6-2-27, Roppongi
Minato-ku, Tokyo
Japan 106

Sigma Design, Inc.
7306 S. Alton Way
Englewood, CO 80112

Sipos, Joseph S.
253 West 15th Street #39
New York, NY 10011

Spectragraphics
10260 Sorrento Valley Road
San Diego, CA 92121

Squires, James A.
Chromatics, Inc.
3331 Ocean Park Blvd., Suite 102
Santa Monica, CA 90405

State University Groningen
Nijenborgh 16
9747 AG Groningen
The Netherlands

Swanson Analysis Systems, Inc.
P.O. Box 65
Houston, PA 15342

TRICAD
1655 McCarthy Blvd.
Milpitas, CA 95035

University of California,
   San Francisco
Computer Graphics Laboratory
San Francisco, CA 94143

University of Houston
4800 Calhoun
Houston, TX 77004

Walter Associates, Inc.
716 South Olive Street
Los Angeles, CA 90014

Zweigler, Mark
CBS Venture One
22-08 Route 208
Fair Lawn, NJ 07410